BALI

Photographs by P.F. Bentley and L.A. Lueras

Text by Elizabeth V. Reyes

Designed by Leonard Lueras

First Edition 1987

TIMES EDITIONS

This page: *Pura Besakih, Bali's mother temple high on the slopes of the sacred mountain Gunung Agung, is silhouetted against a night of* purnama *or full moon. Towering, multi-roofed shrines called* meru *reach toward the heavens here and there on the grounds of important temple sites.*

Following pages: *Bali's religious culture consists of communal sharing of an intricate sequence of annual rites and ceremonies. At one major festival women flood a temple ground, bearing elaborate* banten *offerings of fruit, flowers and ricecakes; yet another group prays together before a temple altar; and young* rejang *dancers at Pura Puseh at Selumbung in east Bali weave across an inner temple courtyard filled with festival goers.*

Contents

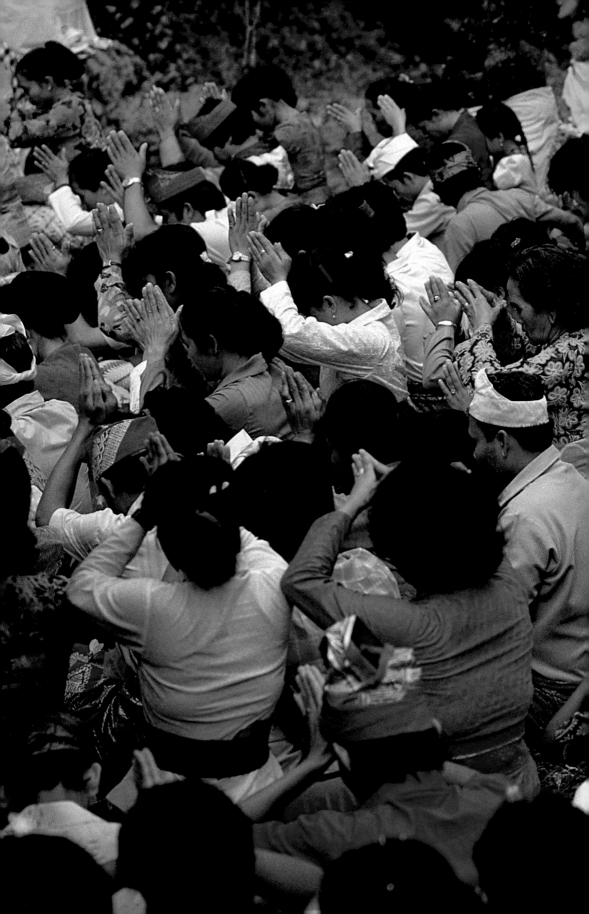

Bali

A Universe Unto Itself

From their tiered heavens above Mount Agung, the Balinese gods keep watch on the perpetual pageant of mortals unfolding below. The afternoon light illuminates a graceful pastoral scene. Decorated bamboo poles called *penjor* line the roads leading to an open air temple set in a knot of villages among the rice *padi*. Colorful parades of village women, all wearing their finest sarongs and brocade sashes, appear on the pathway. On erect heads the women carry towering offerings of food, fruit and flowers. The rose-tinted rice cakes, rows of oranges, bananas and other confections are piled up artistically to a meter in height and crowned with bright blossoms and delicate palm leaf cutwork.

Inside the temple grounds the lavish headdresses are arrayed within a central pavilion. The women kneel for a short prayer service led by an old priest dressed in white. There are ancient chants and pious hand gestures. The aroma of incense and flower blossoms fills the air. Gentle bell-like *gamelan* music from the bronze percussion orchestra starts to permeate the ritualistic proceedings.

Then the temple's colored banners and tall, tasseled umbrellas are assembled for a grand procession. The much-revered resident deity, the glittering leonine Barong, is borne respectfully by two attendants and escorted out of the temple surrounded by his own priests and assistants. The tinkling *gamelan* music changes into a low, hypnotic processional rhythm as the entourage slowly parades down the road into the late afternoon glow, on its way to rendezvous with another such entourage gliding its way towards them. The shimmering pageant is an *odalan*, a one-to seven-day celebration held in commemoration of a temple birthday. Festive and elaborately colorful, the ceremony has remained virtually unchanged for centuries. With at least 30,000 temples of all sizes on the island, such festivities are a daily happening. The pageant of the *odalan* is the essence of Balinese celebration.

Bali is a resplendent medieval Asian tapestry undulating in the 20th century with a way of life that is exotic, aesthetic and full of spectacle. A simple ceremony held in an open air temple stirs an exhilarating rhythm and the languid Balinese dance along in their own elegant and inimitable way.

More than just a place, Bali is an Experience: an experience of whichever part of the pageant a visitor chooses to explore. More than most cultures that have become tourist-oriented meccas, Bali, endlessly complicated,

even contradictory, can be experienced profoundly on many different levels.

At one end of the spectrum are those visitors who will never witness an *odalan*. Their brief stay in Bali is a flurry of tourist-oriented highlights and spectaculars, a "paradise in a package". Locked onto a track running from one of the tourist enclaves on the shores of the southern peninsula to various destinations, they cruise through an abridged version of Bali, consisting of radiant cultural showpieces edited to please. Cultural tourism is, after all, Bali's new motivating theme.

One such typical tourist arrives to catch the Bali sunshine, enjoy the lush tropical land-

*Pageantry is a way of life. A temple anniversary celebration, the **odalan**, begins with ritual bathing of religious images (**preceding pages**), and continues as villagers go to a temple (**left**) with sumptuous temple offerings (**above**).*

scape and get a dose of exotic culture. He watches in rapid succession a "Barong and Kris" dance and "Kecak" dance and is impressed by the performances, mostly without comprehending them; he takes the quickie crafts tour that brings him through the art shops displaying silver, woodcarvings, textiles and paintings; there may be a bus ride up the slopes of Mount Agung and a visit to the great temple complex at Besakih; on the way he will

he chanted the very essence of romance: *"The pulse of life in Bali moves with a measured rhythm reminiscent of the sway of an undersea ballet... There is a similar correlation of the elegant and decorative people with the clear-cut extravagant vegetation, of their sensitive temperament with the fertile land."*

This quotation leads us closer to the source of the cycle of Balinese pageants, to the warm, pungent and fertile earth.

see the terraces of rice *padi* like giant steps linking the river valleys to the highlands. The vendors flog him souvenirs with fervor; he buys wood carvings and a souvenir Barong mask and returns to the hotel, utterly charmed by the "artist's paradise".

At the other end of the spectrum are the "Bali-philes", longer-term visitors or residents who crave a deeper experience and who remain to explore and absorb. With endless patience they follow the *odalan*. They intellectualize over the magic of Bali and the fairy-tale way of life. They search voraciously for the motivation behind the beauty and theatricality of the Balinese people.

The much-quoted father figure of those who have fallen under the spell of the island was the artist and social chronicler, Miguel Covarrubias. Covarrubias made his home in Bali in the 1930s and in his book, *The Island of Bali*,

Within the Indonesian necklace of islands — almost 14,000 strung out between the Southeast Asian mainland and Australasia — Bali is the emerald trinket, suspended about midway down, just south of the equator, and dangling three kilometers off Java's eastern shore. It is one of 27 provinces of Indonesia, a Hindu enclave surrounded by a Muslim nation and a repository of ancient Hindu-Javanese culture. The Balinese are only one of Indonesia's 300 ethnic groups and their language is one of 250 spoken in the country.

The natural beauty of Bali's landscape is legendary. Within the island's 5,632 square kilometers are majestic mountains, fertile hills cut by deep river gorges and long, sandy beaches ringed by coral reefs. Running across the central-northern region is a range of semi-active volcanoes. The highest and most revered of the peaks is Gunung Agung, rising

3,142 meters above sea level. The holy mountain is called "the navel of the world".

Even today many of the 2.6 million inhabitants regard their charmed, compact island as a universe unto itself. To them, Bali is the world and being Balinese is considered an exclusive privilege. Outsiders are labeled "Jaba" or "Java", a term originally reserved for Javanese neighbors but extended to include all non-Balinese. The Balinese regard

priests who had wandered over from Java to sow the seeds of philosophy.

In the year 1343 the island's destiny emerged with the arrival of the Hindu Javanese Majapahit Empire on its shores. The revered General Gajah Mada subjugated the local king and established the new Majapahit court at Gelgel. The land was divided among the conquerors, the holy temple of Pura Besakih was made the Mother Temple, and

the mountains as the home of the gods. Heaven is believed to be an exact reflection of the lovely Balinese landscape, but the sea is dangerous, the dwelling place of demons, monsters and other evil beings. Thus, unlike most islanders, the Balinese are only nominally fisherman. The majority are farmers living in exquisite balance between the mountains and the sea, tilling the soil of the terraced hills.

The Balinese are a Malayo-Polynesian people whose ancestors began migrating from southern China over 2,000 years ago. The island proved a good choice, blessed as it is by fertile soil and protected by a rugged coastline. The coral reefs and treacherous currents sheltered the islanders from foreign interference, thus allowing the Balinese the tranquility to cultivate their rice and their religion. For centuries the Balinese knew no outsiders save some hardy Chinese traders and a few Hindu

Bali began to absorb the culture and ways of the Javanese conquerors.

Over the next 150 years, as Islam took hold in Java, Hindu courtiers continued to migrate eastward to Bali. Herein was the cream of the most civilized race of Java, the Wong Majapahit, a totally new gene-pool of nobles and priests who brought intact their art, religion and philosophy. The Balinese adopted the art of their neighbors, combining it with their raw and earthy forms into a rich and highly expressive style. By the middle of the 16th century, the Gelgel dynasty had achieved the height of imperial and cultural power. This was the Golden Age of classical Balinese

"...thus the gods had ordained — the island was theirs and only given to men on loan..." Balinese regard the mountains as the home of the highest deities. **Above,** *Mount Batur, Lake Bratan and Mount Agung as seen from near Kalimantan.*

Gunung Agung, Bali's Mount Olympus and the heavenly home of the gods, erupted in 1963 in one of the most violent natural catastrophes of this century. Sanghyang Widi Wasa, or Tintia (**left**), is Bali's Supreme God. It is inside Gunung Agung's crater (**below**) that he and other major deities reside.

Gunung Agung

Bali is dominated by Gunung Agung, the holy mountain revered as the "navel of the world".

On a clear day, from almost anywhere on the island, its brooding outline is visible, rising 3,142 meters in the east, over the terraced slopes of rice padi. The highest in a chain of volcanoes that runs east to west across the island, Mount Agung is literally the source of life as well as a source of death. From it comes the life-giving streams that water the fields and the fertile volcanic soil that nourishes the land. From the same mountain comes fire, lava and ashes that can destroy violently — as Gunung Agung did, when it erupted unexpectedly in March 1963.

This majestic mountain embodies both primordial forces and sacred symbolism, and is the holy abode of the gods. The Bali-Hindu religion regards high places as home of the deities and as synonymous with sacredness and purity. In heaven, at the summit of Agung, dwells the supreme god, Sanghyang Widi Wasa, in all his manifestations. Some 900 meters up the slope stands the complex of Pura Besakih, the "Mother Temple". Here, at Bali's most sacred spot, offerings are made to the deities and spirits of the ancestors who reside here on high.

Daily life is continuously affected by Mount Agung. It is the reference point for all directions. Towards the mountain is called kaja, meaning sacred, which is "north" for the majority of Balinese who live to the south, but "south" to those on the north coast. Away from the holy mountain, or towards the sea, is called kelod, meaning profane. This kaja-kelod or sacred-profane concept is ingrained in the Balinese psyche. Villages, temples and house compounds are aligned kaja-kelod, and every village has a temple dedicated to Mount Agung, located in the corner closest to the volcano.

One of the most violent volcanic eruptions of this century took place when the "Supreme Mountain" erupted in 1963. Mount Agung had been lying dormant for over 120 years and was thought to be inactive, its last eruption reported in 1843. That the 1963 eruption of the mountain occurred during the purification ceremony of Eka Dasa Rudra was perceived as having great prophetic importance.

The Eka Dasa Rudra, the most important ritual of purification and sacrifice, is held once every Balinese century. Dedicated to the 11 (eka dasa) sacred directions of the world, it is conducted to restore the harmony between the forces of nature and man. This island-wide ritual of cleansing focussed its activities in Pura Besakih. Just as the most important ceremony was beginning, the holy mountain erupted violently, just above the worshipers.

The first ominous signs of volcanic activity came in mid-February 1963. Within the week, lava started streaming down the mountain's north flank. On March 17 the eruption reached its zenith. A cloud of dense, compressed smoke and ash rose to 10 kilometers above the fomenting crater.

Thick showers of ash affected Singaraja, Bali's northern capital; Surabaya in east Java; and even the republic's capital, Jakarta, 1,000 kilometers away. Lava and mud flows destroyed much of East Bali, burying bridges, roads, fields, and entire villages. After a temporary calm, Agung exploded anew on May 16, spewing intermittently until June 20 — a total of four months of volcanic destruction.

All of Bali was affected. The delicate balance between food supply and population was disrupted. Some 22 per cent of the agricultural land was damaged. Over 1,000 persons were killed and 140,000 left homeless, their temples and agricultural lands buried beneath ash and mud.

Because of the religious reverence accorded to Agung, the eruption doubly affected Balinese society. The very coincidence of the 1963 catastrophe with the Eka Dasa Rudra was both earth and heaven-shaking. Many interpreted it as divine retribution for the past sins of the people. Accepting the natural calamity as punishment by the deities on high, they looked upon the eruption with a strange fatalism, and simply awaited death passively in their homes beneath the angry holy mountain.

Although the sacred Pura Besakih complex stands only about seven kilometers from the crater, it suffered little damage from the eruption. Lava flows seemed to split at the holy ground, avoiding the Mother Temple. The ceremony of Eka Dasa Rudra was mounted anew 16 years later in 1979. The new century was hailed, and the Supreme Mountain has been slumbering peacefully ever since.

culture, a medieval society which was later propulsed into the 20th century.

Most of the Balinese were farmers who lived a remarkably refined and unified pattern of life, integrating agricultural, social and religious aspects into a complex, self-sufficient, interlocking order. Civic life was dominated by the *banjar*, an informal village council of elders concerned with local affairs, family-related matters and the rites of passage celebrated in Balinese life, who also administered village justice. The *subak*, an agricultural society, controlled irrigation and water rights and ensured the equal distribution of the vital water supply to the rice terraces. Both institutions have survived the eroding onslaught of the 20th century and continue to play key roles in everyday village life.

Alongside the agricultural system, there evolved an intricate social order based on traditional rites and customs called *adat*. An individual's role in the community was defined by a series of rituals marking every important stage of life, from birth to death and cremation. Respect for various castes was designated by the use of three "levels" of language. The customs were extended to include precise regulations for building, whereby the proportions of a temple, a house, or family compound, were derived from man's own. The reference point for directions was Mount Agung, the mountain home of the Balinese gods. Everything had a place and a purpose in the complex fabric of life.

The historian Willard A. Hanna, in his book, *Bali Profile*, wrote that the Balinese *"really lives his culture, which compresses into one esthetic package, his life, his work, his social involvements, his religious practices, and his artistic self-fulfillment"*. He added that *"for 1000 years this culture satisfied all his needs... this culture of gem-like beauty and value, such as has rarely, if ever, been matched by any other people"*.

While the villages were self-contained, agricultural communities managed by the *banjar* and *subak* and advised by priests, the rajas and the gentry (about 10 per cent of the population) concerned themselves with pomp and circumstance, with manners, status, the arts and the politics of prestige. During the long pre-20th century history, the rajas' courts

Wayang style paintings, such as this one at Sebatu, derived from two-dimensional shadow puppets brought here from India via Java. These characters usually portray stories from the Hindu Ramayana and Mahabharata epics.

played a splendidly important role in the development of Balinese dance, drama, art and religion. In his fascinating book, *Split Gate to Heaven*, author Rudolf Mrazek records:

"The rulers were patrons of the arts. They favored actors and musicians, exempted them from taxes and treasured them as jewels of the realm. Court life was a continuous flow of ritual extravagance. The best artists were engaged and the whole country was invited to watch them, along with the king. Art filled the courts so absolutely and involved the people flowing through the palace gates so intensely, that the main function of the kingdom appeared to be art. The state moved to music. The public tax went largely for mass rituals... Dance was power, and it was inevitably part of every prince's education to learn several dances in a supremely professional manner, as well as the art of carving, playing gamelan music, and reciting or singing classical verses."

By the end of the 16th century, the Gelgel dynasty had dissolved into a loose grouping of eight independent kingdoms who ruled and fought each other until the coming of the Dutch. The royal families, polygamously inter-married, were prone to jealousy, intrigue and family feuds. The patterns of power and politics became incomprehensible even to the Balinese, as military power passed from the south-central state (Klungkung) to the north (Buleleng) and then east (Karangasem).

In 1597 the ships of Dutchman Cornelius de Houtman stumbled upon Bali during their search for spices. The reports of courtly Balinese life, sent back to Holland by the

In Trunyan, a Bali aga — or original Balinese — village, the dead are not cremated, but left to decompose (above). Right, a grand icon of a monkey king is evidence of the island's pre-Hindu beliefs. Painting by I Made Budi of Batuan.

crew, fired the imagination of the West. But the Dutch were seeking spices, not culture, so Bali was spared the intrusion of the Western world for another two centuries.

By the early years of the 19th century Dutch officials were sending trade missions from their headquarters in Batavia to negotiate with the feisty and eccentric rajas. In 1846 conflicting claims over ship salvage rights brought on the punitive might of the Dutch forces, and by 1884 the northern regencies of Bali were under Dutch control. The southern kingdoms would not be able to hold out for long.

The end came in a gruesome way with a series of mass ritual suicides, *puputan*. Three rajas who had withstood Dutch encroachment preferred self-destruction to the dishonor of surrender. In 1906, with his palace burning behind him, the Raja of Badung (now Denpasar), his court and family, marched into the lines of the Dutch armed forces, ritually killing themselves in a frenzy of death before the shocked and horrified eyes of the soldiers. In 1908 a final *puputan* marked the end of Balinese independence — and, some say, the end of classical Balinese culture.

Between the *puputan* of 1906 and 1908 and the call for independence in the 1940s, Bali was under Dutch control. Fortunately, colonial rule was marked by benevolent and ethical policies and the first gestures towards preserving Balinese culture were made. Perhaps because of the very horror of the *puputan*, the Balinese were spared the harsher policies implemented in those places where the Dutch had strong commercial interests. Western missionaries were discouraged, or even prohibited, from settling on the island.

These were years of social growth and artistic revival. After more than six centuries of court-oriented entertainment, the royals relinquished their cultural domination and the creative arts went back to the villagers and the *banjar*, giving rise to many of the art forms of "modern" Balinese culture.

The post-rajadom era can also be labeled "The Age of Art and Anthropology". By the 1930s Balinese culture was being discovered, examined, recorded and influenced by a bevy of scholars and artists. Walter Spies, a German artist and musician, played a key role in art and painting. Mexican artist Miguel Covarrubias wrote the first examination of Balinese life and his book, *The Island of Bali*, remains a timeless socio-cultural "bible". Colin McPhee, an American ethno-musicologist, wrote the first study of Balinese music. Anthropologists Margaret Mead and Gregory Bateson were

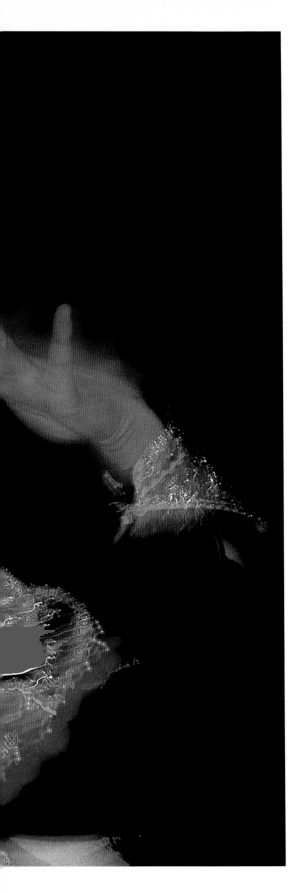

joined by Jane Belo in analyzing and describing the Balinese way of life. Covarrubias wrote perceptively that the newly-discovered 'last paradise' became "*the contemporary substitute for the 19th century romantic conception of primitive Utopia, until then the exclusive monopoly of Tahiti and other South Seas islands*".

In 1931 Bali was dancing for the world, literally, when a troupe from the town of Peliatan, near Ubud in central Bali, performed in Paris. The villages of Ubud, Batuan and Sanur experienced a renaissance in painting as traditional subjects were replaced by scenes of everyday life. The change was due to the influence of the Romantic artist and musician Walter Spies. It is suggested that under his influence, along with that of the Dutch painter Rudolf Bonnet, Balinese art made a quantum leap from the medieval to the modern.

But the revival was interrupted by World

War II, the Japanese Occupation and then the struggle for Indonesian independence, officially declared in 1945 but followed by another four years of disorder. Disasters continued to beleaguer the island in the 1950s and 1960s — a generally poor economy; a plague of rats that caused famine, disease and disruption; the horrific eruption of Mount Agung in 1963 which devastated a quarter of the island and killed over a thousand people; and, in 1965, a nationwide bloodbath in the wake of a nationwide Communist scare that did not leave Bali unscathed. The fragile Balinese world seemed to require the spilling of blood in order to clear the path to a bright future.

Preceding pages: A Segara, Tabananan, wall relief and a brayut *wood sculpture by Ida Bagus Tilem. In the Baris dance (left) a young warrior prepares for war, while in the Kebyar Trompong (above), an artiste dances and plays pots simultaneously.*

The Legong is the heavenly dance of divine nymphs **(below)** which was inherited from the repertoire of 16th century Balinese court rituals. A modern day Balinese bride and bridesmaid from Tabanan **(right)** are glittering princesses of the household for a day.

Classical Legong

Of all Bali's exotic array of storybook dances and dramas the classical Legong is the most popular and best recognized dance with both the Balinese and Bali aficianados. Here is the archetype of femininity, delicacy and refinement — a courtly dance of heavenly nymphs, the Legongs.

During the years of the rajadoms, the Legong dance was performed as a lengthy and lavish entertainment for the lord and his court.

Only the most lithe and graceful adolescent maidens of the land, aged between eight and 12, performed the intense, vibrant dance, accompanied by the haunting and hypnotic rhythm and sounds of intricately beautiful gamelan music.

The most popular number in the long repertoire today is the Legong Kraton. Generally, a much shorter version of the original is presented as the sparkling high note of a five-or six-part dance revue at temple festivals or tourist shows. It is always a dazzling concoction. Three petite girls, elaborately swathed in gold brocade and shimmering frangipani headdresses, float delicately over the floor in a captivating dance of stylized precision.

It is said that the classical Legong was formalized about 150 years ago. It was believed to derive from two existing dance ritual traditions.

The first, the sanghyang dedari, is a trance ritual of purification and exorcism. The "fairy spirit" of the dedari is transformed into stylized movements based on imitations of nature — the bending movement of a tree weighed down with flowers, fluttering dragonfly gestures and the movement of gentle deer being tormented by flies! The dramatic presentation and musical score were taken from the Gambuh dance-drama tradition, a form harking back to the 14th century Hindu-Javanese Majapahit period. What was originally performed by flute music is now a more complex gamelan ensemble which coordinates perfectly with the dancing girls.

The story performed in the Legong Kraton derives from a legend adopted from East Java in the 12th and 13th centuries. The King of Lasem kidnaps the maiden princess, Rangkesari. The Prince of Daha demands her release and threatens war. But the king, though entreated by the princess for her freedom, leaves her and goes to battle.

On the way to this royal confrontation he encounters a tiny bird which delivers a prediction of his death in the forthcoming fight.

The drama is enacted in dance by three exquisite legongs. The servant legong, called the condong, sets the stage with her virtuoso solo dance. Her two heavenly mistresses follow, receive their fans, and spin gossamer circles of movement. The two dancers are mirror images of each other.

At some subtle, almost invisible point, the lithe young girls assume their dramatic character roles, acting out in stylized pantomime the ancient story of chase, abduction, love and war.

Yet what matters most is not the story but the performance itself. The essence of the legong is the gilded form, not the ancient tale. Balinese dance connoisseurs look for the choreographic precision, the harmony of gestures and the perfectly-timed gamelan music. Over and over again the Legong thrills entranced audiences with its dazzling intensity.

A young theater troupe that specializes in the ancient and classical Gambuh, *an operatic dance-drama of the 14th century, thrives and continues to tell the tradition-bound stories today in the village of Batuan. A large number of local cultural societies and village religious tenets keep such theatric traditions flourishing across this artistically rich and enchanting island.*

A carved stone frieze on a northern Bali temple wall (including modern images like airplanes, a bicycle and a Japanese soldier) depicts the traumatic coming of World War II to Bali. Folk carvings on the "baroque" temples to the north of the island often picture a strong visual evidence of an hybrid culture.

Historical Chronology

6th century — A traveling Chinese Buddhist monk describes the island of "Po'li", believed to be Bali, as composed of some 136 villages set amid luxurious vegetation and ruled by a king believed to be a descendant of Hindu deities.

882 — The oldest dated inscription in Bali records the first king ruling Bali as Ugrasena, founder of the Warmadewa Dynasty.

Late 10th century — The island of Bali is conquered by the Javanese king Dharmawangsa (989-1007). His sister, Princess Mahendradatta, marries the Balinese king, Udayana.

1001 — Prince Erlangga is born. Son of the king Udayana and princess Mahendradatta, Erlangga returns to Java where he builds a powerful kingdom, rules Bali as part of his empire and lays the foundations of Javanese-Balinese contact.

Early 12th century — Bali becomes a vassal of the eastern Javanese kingdom of Kediri.

1284 — The neighboring Javanese ruler, Kertanegara, re-conquers, pacifies and unifies Bali under the Singasari Dynasty.

1343 — Gajah Mada, Supreme General and Prime Minister of the Majapahit Empire, conquers Bali and introduces the Majapahit culture and its institutions. The Balinese are most receptive and the aristocracy eagerly seek to join their family trees to the ruling "Wong Majapahit".

1450 — The Hinduization of Bali proceeds through waves of migration and cultural infusion from the Majapahit Empire in Java.

1515 — The collapse of the Majapahit Empire (with the unstoppable rise of Islam) triggers a massive cultural migration to Bali. The last prince of Majapahit and his royal court of Hindu priests, artists, scholars, nobles and soldiers flee to Bali, transferring their culture intact.

1550 — Batu Renggong of the Gelgel Dynasty inherits the title of Dewa Agung, Great Deity or King, and initiates a political, military and cultural renaissance sometimes called Bali's "Golden Age". He controls all the Balinese rajadoms and conquers Sumbawa and Lombok. Several generations later the family dynasty moves its court to Klungkung, which remains the "noblest" of the eight rajadoms or principalities. (These rajadoms are: Klungkung, Badung, Tabanan, Bangli, Gianyar, Karangasem, Buleleng and Jembrana).

1597 — The earliest Dutch trader, Cornelius de Houtman, arrives in Bali, searching for spices. Four members of the expedition are royally entertained by the court of Gelgel. Two men jump ship for the pleasures of tropical Bali, and the Western world receives fascinating reports about the island.

1601 — A Dutch expedition, led by Jacob van Heemskerck, tries to open trade with the island. The Dewa Agung presents him with a beautiful Balinese girl slave; and the Dutch interpret this as

bestowing special rights upon them.

1639 — Di Made Bekung, last Dewa Agung of the "Golden Age" of the Gelgel Dynasty, provokes an invasion of Bali by the Javanese Empire of Mataram. He loses Sumbawa and Lombok and the allegiance of the other Balinese princes. The Gelgel court moves to Klungkung. They continue to symbolize Hindu imperial grandeur, but never again have real imperial power.

1667 — The rajadom of Gianyar is born with the rise of Dewa Manggis Kuning, a fourth generation Gelgel. After early misadventures in Badung, Dewa Manggis escapes arrest — by being carried out of the palace wrapped in a woven mat carried atop an old servant's head. The fugitive prince sets up a Gianyar court which eventually becomes a prosperous and powerful southern state.

1711 — The Dewa Agung's military and political power passes to Buleleng in the north. The joint rajadom of Buleleng-Mengwi flourishes for the better part of the 18th century.

1717–1718 — Frequent hostilities between Bali and the Javanese Empire of Mataram climax in the destruction of East Java and Madura by roaming Balinese troops. The Dutch refrain from real intervention in the Balinese-Javanese wars.

1740 — The rajadom of Karangasem rises to prominence when it conquers Lombok. Raja Gusti Gede Karangasem, a famous figure in Balinese history, subdues Buleleng, then Negara as well, dominating the political scene and stirring the populace to widespread resentment and anger.

1815 — Tambora Volcano on Sumbawa erupts. Buleleng and Singaraja, the large towns of north Bali, are damaged by ash and tidal waves. This is taken as a premonition of disaster.

1817 — The Dutch begin agricultural trade with Bali. Singaraja and Kuta become busy ports.

1826 — A permanent Dutch agent settles in Kuta, South Bali, beginning modern Dutch presence on the island. Captain J.S. Wetters' purpose is to recruit 1000 Balinese soldiers for the Dutch colonial army. The trade in opium and Balinese slaves flourishes under his influence.

1830s — Dutch traders begin to negotiate trade policies and sovereignty. The Balinese hold to a traditional concept of reef rights whereby villagers are entitled to plunder any ship that comes to grief near the island, accepting it as a gift of the gods.

1841 — The Dutch frigate *Overijsset* is wrecked on the Kuta reef and plundered of its cargo by Balinese. Amid furor and protest, a new Dutch commissioner lands at Buleleng. He is defied by a dramatic, dynamic young prince, Gusti Ketut Jelantik, the great hero of mid-19th century Bali.

1846 — Dutch-Bali wars. The first Dutch punitive

expedition brings an invasion fleet of 58 vessels and 3000 well-armed men to defeat Jelantik's defense force in Buleleng. Danish trader Mads Lange, who runs a successful shipping and trading post in Kuta, acts as an intermediary and tries to negotiate a truce between the rajas and the Dutch.

1848 — In the second Dutch punitive expedition the brilliant military leader Gusti Jelantik fights off three attacks with 25 cannon and 16,000 men.

1849 — The third and final Dutch expedition arrives with 100 armed vessels. The Dutch attack the Balinese stronghold at Jagaraga. The Balinese lose thousands, then advance in *puputan* (ritual suicide). The Dutch gain allies and troops from Lombok, who overtake the rajas of Karangasem and Buleleng. The Balinese resistance is in complete disarray whilst the Dutch get stronger.

1850s — The Dutch "protective" administration assumes sovereign power over northern and western Bali. A new coffee plantation turns the north into a profitable colonial enterprise. Dutch ban the Hindu practice of *suttee*, the burning of widowed wives with their husbands, and take the first enlightened steps to wipe out slavery.

1868 — As the climax to the intermittent Gianyar-Klungkung wars, the rajadom of Gianyar, the most prosperous and powerful state of the south, shatters the Klungkung army.

1882 — Buleleng and Jembrana states are brought under direct Dutch rule. All Balinese women in that part of the island are ordered to cover their breasts.

1885 — The Dewa Manggis and his Gianyar retinue travel to Klungkung to pay homage to the Dewa Agung, but they are imprisoned instead and their ranks are destroyed. A rebellion of Muslim Sasaks in Lombok, vassals of the Balinese rulers of Karangasem, East Bali, is suppressed with cruelty.

1894 — The Dutch send a military expedition to Lombok to punish the Balinese rulers, but they are ambushed and massacred in the notorious "Lombok Treachery", at their camp in Cakranegara. To revenge their defeat, the Dutch lay to waste Lombok Island and raze Mataram to the ground in the process. The Balinese nobles perish in the mass rite of *puputan*, or ritual suicide, rather than surrender to the invaders. Dutch-Balinese relations are increasingly strained.

1900 — The Dutch annex the rajadom of Gianyar.

1904 — The Chinese schooner *Sri Kumala* is wrecked near Sanur beach and is plundered. The Dutch demand compensation from the raja of Badung, who remains defiant — and is backed up by the rajas of Klungkung and Tabanan. The last *suttee* takes place in Tabanan this year.

1906 — A large Dutch military expedition lands at Sanur beach and troops march towards the royal

In the 1930s, when Balinese culture was being "rediscovered" by the world's literati, artists, musicologists and anthropologists, one of the island's star attractions was a young dancer named I Mario. Mario, who hailed from the east Bali town of Tabanan, was renowned as a dancer and musician. In the picture below he is shown performing his specialty, the highly-stylized kebyar dance.

palace in Denpasar. They are met by the raja and his entire court, splendidly dressed for the tragic rite of *puputan*. In a ghastly suicide ceremony, the company turn their daggers and kris upon one another. The women tauntingly throw jewels at the Dutch soldiers. The entire court dies together and the battlefield before the burning palace is covered with mounds of corpses. The *puputan* ritual is repeated that same afternoon in Pemecutan, a minor court of Badung; and two days later in the court of the raja of Tabanan.

1908 — Disorder and bombardment around Gelgel and Klungkung lead to the final *puputan* of the Dewa Agung and his court in Klungkung, the victims of relentless western intrusion. The Dutch resolve to make amends. They introduce reforms under the Ethical Policy. They do not allow the presence of a Dutch colony, nor agricultural business, as in Java. Balinese farmers are protected against large-scale western exploitation and against the sudden impact of outside influences. A "conservationist" stance towards Balinese culture is taken and Dutch scholars usher in an era of distinguished achievements in art and architecture.

1920s–1930s — Foreign scholars, artists and musicians "discover" Bali. They record it and broadcast it to the world. Among the visitors are anthropologists Margaret Mead, Jane Belo and Gregory Bateson; artists Miguel Covarrubias, Walter Spies,

Rudolf Bonnet, Ari Smit, Han Snel; musician Colin McPhee; writer Vicki Baum; and dancers Ted and Katharine Mershon.

1942 — Japanese Occupation. Japanese troops land at Sanur beach and control the island for three years, through headquarters at Denpasar and Singaraja. Walter Spies, Bali's most famous Western artist, perishes when a Japanese submarine torpedoes the ship on which he is being transported to safety as a German internee.

1945 — General Sukarno, a soldier and politician who has risen fast through the party ranks in Jakarta, declares *Merdeka* — Independence — for all the Indonesian archipelago. Dutch troops drive the Japanese out of Bali and try to reimpose a Dutch civil administration.

1946 — The battle for independence on Bali climaxes with the Margarana Incident in Tabanan state. A charismatic young Balinese military officer, Ngurah Rai — who relies not on tactics and logistics but upon intuition and mystical guidance — leads a suicide attack against Dutch forces and is martyred at Marga along with 95 followers.

1949 — The Hague concedes Indonesian independence. Bali becomes part of the Republic of the United States of Indonesia.

1956 — Sukarno, President of Indonesia and "patron" of Bali island, builds various monuments such as the opulent Tampaksiring Palace, the bun-

During a break in rest and business, U.S. President Ronald Reagan and Indonesia's President Soeharto pause to toast each other's wives. While their husbands discussed economic issues, Mrs. Nancy Reagan and Mrs. Tien Soeharto visited a Balinese compound, enjoyed a high tea, and laughed together as Mrs. Reagan tried her hand at Balinese dancing.

ker-like Bali Beach Hotel, and Udayana University, which is now Bali's chief center of higher education.

1962 — A plague of rats infests Bali's fields and granaries. This is interpreted as a divine signal of the displeasure of the deities.

1963 — Gunung Agung, the holiest mountain, revered as the "Navel of the World", suddenly erupts without warning, killing over a thousand people and laying much of the island to waste. This volcanic catastrophe occurs while the Balinese are busy celebrating Eka Dasa Rudra, the most sacred of festivals, held only once every Balinese century at Pura Besakih, the mother temple on the slopes of Gunung Agung. The eruption is read as an evil omen, a sign of divine retribution.

1965 — Gestapu, the September 30 incident in Jakarta, is an abortive coup d'etat; five top army generals are brutally mutilated by a clique of communist conspirators. Popular revulsion and desire for vengeance promotes a national blood-letting. In Bali thousands of suspected communists are killed in a matter of weeks.

1970s — Tourism develops in south Bali, in the capital city Denpasar and in the beach resort villages of Sanur and Kuta. The Ngurah Rai International Airport in Tuban is opened. The government declares tourism the new industry and launches the development of the Nusa Dua mega-resort in the Bukit Peninsula.

1979 — On January 31st, in what in recent years has been called "the last great cremation", the remains of the Tjekorde Gde Agung Sukawati, the High Prince and would-have-been Rajah of Ubud, were burned in a huge black and gold bull sarcophagus. The *Bali Post* newspaper estimated that some 100,000 people attended this cremation which involved six months of preparation (by some 2,500 people) and cost an estimated 75 million rupiahs (or about US$120,000. 1The *Bali Post* called this ritual royal burn "one of Ubud's most ostentatious displays of ceremonial ritual in this decade".

1979 — Balinese island-wide again celebrate Eka Dasa Rudra on Mount Agung. Exactly 11 years and 11 days after the aborted festival of 1963, this massive celebration — involving the most elaborate preparations and animal sacrifices ever — is pronounced a success: the successful purging of the old and the blessed beginning of a new century of hope to the Balinese people.

1986 — American President Ronald Reagan, his wife, Nancy, and a host of other U.S. diplomats arrived here on April 29th to meet with Indonesia's President Soeharto and the foreign ministers of the six Asean countries. As the Reagan entourage stepped off Air Force One at Ngurah Rai Airport, they were garlanded with flowers and greeted by President Suharto and a troupe of Balinese dancers. The U.S. President was on the island for four days.

For all the massive upheavals of modern history, Balinese culture has survived intact and seems to have transcended time itself. The feature that most fascinates visitors and researchers today — more than stunning landscape or lush terraces of rice *padi* or even the gilded history of the rajas and their courts — is the unique religious culture that still thrives, manifested vividly in everyday worship. Balinese religion, entwined with economics, is the basis of the social order and the motivating force behind the picturesque way of life. Contemporary authors have called this Balinism: the social, aesthetic and religious practice of 90 per cent of the Balinese people. Balinism is the endless medieval pageant lived daily in the tranquil villages.

The roots of Balinism are to be found in age-old animistic beliefs from a time when the island world was filled with forces beyond man's control and understanding. Balinese man placed his fragile fate in the hands of superior beings and created a pantheon of protective spirits governing nature. Man, poised at the very center of this cosmos, believed he could actively gain the goodwill of the gods — and demons — by performing certain rites and sacrifices. Gradually he developed an elaborate system of ceremonies all aimed at keeping the goodwill flowing and maintaining equilibrium among all the forces.

Over several centuries this animist faith evolved into Balinese Hinduism (or more properly Hindu Dharma). As various concepts and ideas arrived via Java, Balinese theology absorbed elements of Mahayanic Buddhism in the seventh century, orthodox Sivaism in the ninth; various tantric beliefs through the 11th; and finally the Javanized Hinduism of the Majapahit kingdom in the 14th. Religion, like Balinese culture, was syncretic.

The Balinese recognize one supreme creative god, Sanghyang Widhi Wasa, as manifested primarily through the Hindu trilogy of Brahma, Siva and Vishnu, adopted from the huge pantheon of Indian gods and goddesses. But religious practice today includes ancestor worship, belief in evil spirits, blood sacrifices, Brahmanic juggling of mystic words and mantra-like syllables and, most importantly, the cremation of the dead so that the soul will be freed and can live again in the Hindu-Balinese cycle of reincarnation.

Rama and Sita of the classical Ramayana epic strike dance poses before an oil lamp made up of coiled snakes, or nagas. *These traditional characters are usually surrounded by the spectacular dancers-chanters of the all-male* kecak *dance.*

Yet the religion is earth bound. All of these diverse elements have been absorbed, transformed or juggled to suit the Balinese temperament. Wrote Covarrubias: *"The Balinese are a people who never lost contact with the soil; who stayed supreme over the philosophies of the masters... Hinduism was simply an addition to the native religion — a strong but superficial veneer of decorative Hindu practice over a deeply rooted animism."*

The Balinese worship of nature spirits is charming in its practice. The frequent propitiation of unseen deities shapes each day with an alluring rhythm. After the early morning sweeping of the compound yards, a Balinese matron will make her ritual rounds, placing an array of *segehan* (small offerings of rice and flower petals in palm leaf trays) wherever the spirits may pass — in the family temple, by compound walls, in doorways or pathways or

crossroads, to appease the demons of the low places. At each offering the matron pauses, sprinkles holy water and wafts incense. The "essence" rises, the gods "partake" of the food, and dogs eat the material remains!

On other occasions Balinese matrons will take part in the rituals performed on *tumpek* days, days which honor the deities of trees and plants, metals and machines, books, sacred masks and puppets. During the most important festival of the year, called *Galungan*, the calendar overflows with the sacred rites and ceremonies held to placate the visiting spirits.

Wrote the indefatigable chronicler Covarrubias: *"The islanders lead a musical-comedy*

A duck herder of Sebatu (above) tends his waddling flock with the unchanging patience of the centuries. A pious and elderly matron, meanwhile, kneels in devotion while making floral and fruit offerings to the gods of the rice fields (right).

sort of life, full of weird, picturesque rites."

Weird? The average Balinese villager is much too preoccupied to care that the modern world deems his lifestyle odd, quaint or exotic. He spends, by conservative estimate, half of his time and energy on community religious pursuits. He is motivated and held in check by his religion. He always returns home for a festival or family rite. And he is relaxed in his worship and not fanatical. The fine points of theology and philosophy are left to the high priest, the *pedanda*, who speaks directly to the gods in an ancient Sanskrit tongue.

Picturesque? Religion is a participatory expressive experience, a social dimension of life. Balinism is a harmonious way of worship, a "good feeling" of belonging to one's community and having the habit of ceremony. A village *odalan* is *ramai* — bustling, noisy, crowded — involving masses of people. There are food stalls set up outside the temple and medicine hawkers taking advantage of the assembled crowd. The air is festive with *gamelan* music, lavish fruit-and-flower offerings, holy water and prayers. In *odalan* after *odalan* the rhythm of Balinism continues.

Dance is an important part of Balinese life, worship and festivity. *Biyar! Biyar!*... the opening chords of the *gamelan* resound as with gusto a "Barong and Kris" dance begins. Tourists can see a performance in Batubulan, a village just minutes north of the capital, Denpasar. The mythical Barong, a large hairy beast, confronts the evil witch-widow, Rangda, with her fangs bared, great tongue lolling and breasts and entrails hanging. Suddenly a horde of men appear waving kris at the witch and then furiously stab themselves. Neither the jovial Barong, nor the wicked Rangda, seems to win. An uninitiated audience may be impressed by the theatrics but bewildered by the significance of the story.

The performance in Batubulan is but an exciting extract from a lengthier moral drama depicting the eternal battle between good and evil. The Barong is the benefactor and protector. In his real religious persona he is "entered" by the spirit, and performs sacred exorcism rituals within the temple grounds. Borne by two trance mediums, the gold-spangled Barong dances to banish evil and restore order and balance to the community.

Whether one witnesses the island's unique

Padi rice fields (preceding pages) patchwork the gentler slopes of west Bali. Rangda, the ghoulish witch-widow, and Barong, the gilded leonine god and benefactor of mankind (right), are eternal adversaries in the battle of good versus evil.

44

A Balinese wedding entourage, with four brocade-swathed bridesmaids flanking the bride and groom, sits in gilded glory during a Tabanan reception. Earlier, the bridal couple completed the traditional tooth-filing ritual, which oftentimes marks the end of adolescence and the start of adult life. Such ceremonies, like everything else on Bali, are held only on auspicious days.

dance and drama in the tourist showplace or by the village temple gates, the art of theater is alive and well — indeed thriving — as pure entertainment, popular education and religious ritual. The dramas are derived from Hindu mythology, colored by a heavy dose of Balinese inspiration and perfected by centuries of performance under the patronage of the Balinese rajas and the temple communities.

In music, the bronze gongs of the gamelan

deemed to be the island's economic salvation. Marketing a ringside view of their culture in exchange for foreign funds was seen as the best way of expanding the economy. "Only tourism can contribute the multiplier effect necessary for development," reasoned one senior Bali administrator.

Thus began the "packaged paradise" phenomenon, along with a new concept known as "cultural tourism", a formula for development

burst into flamboyant life, spinning a percussive web of sound with hammers that race over 15 paired metal xylophones. This is the bold *kebyar* style of the 20th century. *Kebyar* literally means "to burst forth" or "to bloom suddenly as a flower"; *kebyar* is an onomatopoeic name given to the modern sound of music first heard in north Bali about 1915. Unlike its stately predecessor in the court, this modern gamelan sound is more florid and frenetic, more *ramai* — as busy, crowded and lavish as possible.

From the early 1970s Bali has experienced mass tourism. The charmingly naive culture was made instantly available by jet airliners and package tours. Tourism was declared the "New Industry". With a population growing faster than the rice-based economy, and coupled with a lack of timber, oil and other resources, the return of tourism was

which allows for commercialization without vulgarization. The Indonesian government embarked on an effort to attract international tourists and built a new string of luxury resort hotels in the Nusa Dua Complex, about 30 kilometers from the capital city of Denpasar, to house them. In terms of sight-seeing, this means an aesthetic "package of paradise" in several days, without allowing tourists to affect local life and traditions.

How is tourism influencing the Balinese? Once-tranquil villages have burgeoned with tourist-related commerce along the main roads. Rice farmers with leisure time have turned into small scale businessmen. Artisans try their

Vibrant colors and the graceful movements of the women turn a Denpasar public market into a show as interesting to watch as a festival (left). With a thousand exotic forms and textures, the market is a big village event every third day.

Balinese Food

The first thing a visitor learns about Balinese food is that it is so highly-spiced with pungent roots, leaves, garlic, nuts, fermented shrimp paste, lime juice, grated coconut and burning red peppers, that only adventurous gourmets can appreciate it. The second thing a visitor learns is that it can be rather difficult to obtain the real thing in a tourist town.

For the Balinese themselves, daily dining is a simple affair that takes place in the privacy of the home. A pot of rice and a few modest viands are cooked up early in the morning and consumed through the day with little fanfare. This may be topped off in the evening with some sticks of sate (meat on a skewer), spicy fruit mixtures or nasi campur (rice with whatever) available at the local warung, the foodstalls that are as much a favorite meeting place as a dining table.

Balinese festivities tell a different dining story. A community banquet makes eating and cooking a social affair. The festive table groans under the weight of spicy vegetables, hot soups and dishes of chicken and pork — plus sweet rice cakes and tuak or brem, fermented palm and rice drinks.

It is from the Balinese festive table that Bali's restaurants have derived their limited native fare. Much time is needed to prepare an authentic Balinese meal. Some of the larger, older restaurants in Sanur or Kuta can orchestrate a special Balinese dinner given at least 24 hours' advance notice and preferably the attendance of six to 12 people. Highlights of the dinner are roast suckling pig, smoked or baked duck, steamed spiced pork, sate and several varieties of chopped fresh vegetables to crunch on.

Babi guling, or roast suckling pig, is Bali's national dish. This favorite taste treat consists of a small piglet stuffed with herbs, drenched with coconut oil and cooked whole on a spit.

Traditionally the different parts of the babi are served separately — the crispy golden skin, freshly-roasted meats, plus side portions of pork sausages, crunchy, curly pork rind, fried pork meats. And all with heaps of steamed rice.

The babi of the traditionally-observed festivals is usually accompanied by the spicy lawar, a dish reserved for special occasions. Lawar is a finely chopped medley of vegetables, coconut and slivered meats mixed together with loads of chillis and usually fresh blood. The blood is used to flavor the dish as well as for religious reasons.

Bebek betutu is Bali's famous smoked duck, the hands-down prizewinner of the local cuisine. The duck is marinated, stuffed with herbs and wrapped in banana leaf before it is buried for eight to 10 hours in a slow fire of rice chaff and coconut husks. The duck takes on a subtle, smoky flavor.

Sate is skewered bits of meat barbequed over coals and served with a dark peanut sauce. Besides the usual chicken, pork or mutton sate, familiar throughout the Malay world, Bali has two unique versions, sate penyu, turtle meat, and sate lilit, a pressed concoction of fish or pork blended together with aromatic grated coconut.

Other Balinese dishes to tempt the palate include tum babi, a spiced pork steamed in banana leaf; ikan pepes, baked fish; and in the dessert department, black rice pudding and sweet rice cakes.

hand at the service sector, opening a *losmen* (a small inn), a *warung* (food stall) or offering visitors a "home-stay". Village matrons sell woodcarvings and children hawk postcards. In the larger tourist hubs, Balinese man the international hotels. Some 30,000 are directly employed in the tourism industry.

The Baliphiles, those visitors who stay to follow the *odalan*, sigh as they watch vendors parade towers of cheap sarongs and soft drinks

shows co-exists with a more sedate way of life and has been accepted by the Balinese, whose own culture allows for the co-existence of disparate ideas and practices.

As far back as the 1930s people were asking: 'Is Bali spoiled?' Covarrubias worried about the effects wrought by an influx of foreigners that was a mere one per cent of what it is today. But as the historian Willard Hanna wrote: *"The debate... is futile. The genuine Bali and*

on their heads instead of fruit-and-flower offerings. They lament the proliferation of motorbike shops; regret seeing so-called artists churn out tatty paintings by the dozen; and bewail the "Kuta cowboys", boys who leave family to work in the low-budget *losmen* and hustle the foreign girls.

Yet many Balinese welcome the over 200,000 foreign visitors who come to their island annually. The *"orang turis"* are seen as odd outsiders bearing much desired yen, dollars and pounds, and are accepted with enthusiasm, despite the occasional negative consequence of their presence. The world of hotels, restaurants, tour buses and dance

Motorcars have their own day of celebration too: Tumpek Landep. *Villagers honor the deities of metal with palm-and-flower offerings (above). Boys in Denpasar (right) grow up in an urbanized culture of movies, motorbikes, TV and tourists.*

the authentic Balinese are still to be found.... The Balinese magic still works, which is in itself a reassuring miracle."

In other words, one must look beyond the tourist hubs and seek out life in the temples and villages where the opulent *odalan* still ripple and the Balinese pray.

"People have sometimes been deeply concerned that the tourist boom might destroy Bali's culture," said Bali Tourism Director, Cokorda Oka Pemayun.

"But I'm convinced this won't happen. Why? Because the culture is solidly built. It is like a *bale*, a Balinese house. The foundation is the religion, the base, close to the earth. The traditional institutions of the *subak* and the *banjar* are the pillars of the house, the posts of the Balinese society. And the roof is the culture, sheltering and protecting the society.

"The roof tiles can blow away, yes, but we

Ngurah Rai

I Gusti Ngurah Rai was the quintessential Balinese hero: an impassioned patriot, guerilla activist and inspired army commander whose slogan was "Merdeka Atau Mati" — "Freedom or Death". A charismatic leader who relied not so much on tactics and logistics, but rather on intuition and indeed upon mystical guidance, he was martyred in Marga, West Bali, in 1946, after making Bali's last stand against the Dutch colonial forces.

In 1945, this young military officer, 28, emerged as a leader during the prolonged struggle for independence (Merdeka), when the Japanese, Dutch and Balinese were jockeying for power on the island. A Dutch-educated soldier and a Ksatriya-caste commander with ties to Majapahit ancestry — Ngurah Rai struggled to unify Bali's varied activist bands into a disciplined and effective military force which he called the TKR, the People's Security Force.

His rag-tag, under-armed, under-trained army of up to 1000 men and boys — called a "pack of rabble" by the Dutch — never had more than one modern weapon for every 10 recruits, nor enough ammunition to undertake more than a lightning barrage. In December 1945, Lieutenant Ngurah Rai's TKR band made a concerted raid against the Japanese barracks — an attempt to seize arms which failed. Pursued by patrols, Ngurah Rai and his guerilla aides retreated to Java to seek weapons and reinforcements.

The Balinese soldier-activist was to meet his destiny in 1946. The Dutch forces had occupied Denpasar and started to re-establish the civil administration. On his return from Java, as a Lieutenant-Colonel in charge of the TKI division of the Indonesian Republic Army, commander Ngurah Rai harassed the Dutch over long weeks of raids and ambushes, skirmishes and retreats. His regrouped army now comprised diverse units of Balinese and Javanese — along with some Japanese soldiers who had defected to join the guerillas.

Lt-Col Ngurah Rai's final grand strategy, the famous "Long March to Gunung Agung", unfolded as a heroic but tragic story. The leader rallied all his scattered men in east Bali, taking sanctuary on the slopes of the sacred mountain. He hoped to lure the Dutch forces out and infiltrate their lines by guerilla tactics. But instead, the tables were turned and the people's army found themselves encircled. They fled for their lives, over the hazardous volcanic peak of Gunung Agung and across the mountains to the western region of Tabanan.

Regrouping in Marga on November 18, 1946, Ngurah Rai and his much-depleted band were trapped anew by the reinforced Dutch army. The Dutch called for surrender, but what followed was a massacre, a bloody fight to the end, reminiscent of the puputan of Badung 40 years earlier. Commander Ngurah Rai led his 95 men in a final suicidal attack upon the heavily armed enemy. Their martyrdom marked the end of effective Balinese resistance.

The site of this last battle, called the Margarana Incident, is today designated as a national heroes' cemetery dedicated to all the men and women who died during the Balinese resistance movement. A high-level military ceremony is held there annually.

The memory of the martyred Balinese commander himself lives on in Bali's Ngurah Rai International Airport. A huge bronze statue of the wartime hero, atop a high marble pedestal, towers over the airport crossroad, depicting a cool, dignified, uniformed officer rather than the impassioned guerilla fighter of Merdeka. It is an ironically tranquil monument to the last of Bali's charismatic war heroes — and the very first landmark on the island of Bali to greet modern airborne travelers on arrival.

Behold the Balinese bemo (below), three-wheeled workhorse of the island roads. This mighty mini-truck buzzes madly around town shuttling people and produce from dawn to dusk. During a Balinese *odalan* **(right),** women of the village wear festive finery and prepare grand offerings for presentation to their ancestral gods.

Bemos

The bemo *is the rambling chimera of the Bali road. It races about honking and competing for passengers. But it is a useful beast of burden, moving people and their produce from village to town.*

The term bemo *is derived from two predecessors: the* becak, *Java's old three-wheeled bicycle carriage, and the modern motorcar. The contraction* bemo *was first applied to Bali's motorized three-wheeled mini cabs, which have been plying the Denpasar city runs since the mid-sixties. There are still just over a hundred three-wheelers in town, and a ride across town costs about US12 cents (Rp 125).*

After the "bugs" came the standard four-wheel bemos, *sometimes called "Colts". When these Toyota-made pick-ups arrived around 1973, they superseded the traditional big buses that had ferried people around the island..*

Colts can seat 12 to 14 people face-to-face in the spacious back area, with room for all the produce in between. They may be clumsy looking but are ultra-practical inside. Excess passengers hang off the back step as the Colt speeds on its rounds connecting up the remoter villages.

By the 1980s bemo *had become the nickname for all public vehicles smaller than the lumbering old bus and* bemos *started to multiply and diversify.*

The most colorful bemos *are the mini-cabs, usually Mitsubishi and Suzuki, that look like train carriages. Along the Sanur-Denpasar route, four hundred green, yellow and blue* bemos *beep down the roads collecting a paltry Rp 100 to travel along* the beach streets and Rp 250 to 300 for the longer ride into the city of Denpasar.

Inside the mini cab are two facing benches, raised eight inches off the floor. Adults are folded in knee-to-knee and head-to-ceiling, with doe-eyed children pressed in between.

The bemo *driver's life is hot and tedious. It was a good business about five years ago, but today there is too much competition. The driver and his helper, the* krenet *(which means ticket — there aren't any), collect Rp 8,000 to 9,000 during an average 6 am to 6 pm day. Of that, Rp 5,000 goes to the bemo owner.*

After dark, bemos *ferry people homeward on a private-hire, free-route basis. With darkness falling, and a lack of other options, "vampire" rates of Rp 2,000–3,000 a ride come into effect.*

The most comfortable bemos *today are the up-graded minibuses. These 12-seater passenger coaches have leatherette seats arranged in rows.*

Public minibuses, called stasiuns *(stations) in Denpasar, are named after the depot from whence they take off for points north, east or west. Their price is about 15 per cent more than local cabs, they seat fewer people and their drivers are more relaxed than the downtown* bemo *drivers.*

Finally there is the tourist "transpo't". These high and roomy minibuses are hawked by drivers who have staked their territory near the larger hotels. They seat six to ten tourists with ease and can be chartered for US$25 to $40 a day, depending on the time and place and the skill of the negotiator...

can always replace them. We are always doing spring cleaning! As long as the religion and the *subak* and the *banjar* are there, Bali culture is always sure of its identity."

It is generally the romantic traditionalists, especially Bali's educated gentry, who worry about cultural identity. Cokorda Parta, a descendant of the Peliatan aristocracy, has watched the tourist boom since the mid-sixties and, while he welcomes progress and development, he also says:

"When I think of the negative effects, like the situation at Kuta Beach, for example, I cry. And I worry that this may spread to the villages. I feel no jealousy towards the tourist towns, and I tell my people to keep their name safe, their reputation as a gentle people."

Cokorda, the traditionalist, worries that those under the age of 40 will forget and lose the old customs, knowing only the new com-

mercial ways. He bemoans the low level of education in Bali-Hindu religion, as well as the lack of politeness in tourist enclaves. He lives graciously sheltered in a 16-pillared pavilion and he admits to getting a headache whenever he visits Kuta for an hour.

Kuta Beach. "What a horrible place," winces one hotel developer. "Been there, done that" declares a cynical beach singlet stretched across the shoulders of an Aussie cruising contentedly on a motorbike down Jalan Pantai, in downtown Kuta.

The message is the fad of the season, as is the rider's triangle of white sun cream on the nose and colored plastic beads threaded

Whimsical Hindu, Buddhist and even animist iconography pops up at every turn on this island. A garuda bird and meditative Buddha image glow in an Ubud curio shop (left) and a grotesque demon cavorts on a Sukawati wall (above).

through his ash blond hair, ear to ear. Kuta still means cheap living and good beaches and the Australians have invaded the town to the tune of 85,000 a year. It is fun, funky and ultra-convenient. But negatively it is also dreadfully noisy, crowded with tourists, and a big headache for the Balinese.

Kuta was a laid-back fishing village with just one dusty road down to the flat gray beach up to the 1970s. In those days it was patronized

visit but any visitor with a sensitive soul wouldn't want to live there.

If Kuta is a midnight cowboy, Sanur Beach is a sleepy lady, a lovely place to live, but rather dull to visit. Sanur, a proud old Balinese village now dotted with several large hotels along a serene coral-reefed beach, is languid and gracious. Sanur's sands are soft and golden, the beach less traveled. A tightly knit community, known for colorful, highly-charge

by a few sun freaks who had come to the end of the back-packing trail. Ten years later, Kuta is a raunchy and raucous town with ten times as many beach vendors, perhaps 15 times as many smoke-belching motorbikes and five times as many roads.

Hundreds of family-run *losmen*, *warung* and restaurants have sprouted up and the congestion is working its way north along the beach to Legian and Seminyak, the next villages up the coast. The unplanned settlement is somewhat seedy at the center and rough at the edges. The tourist has all the beer pubs, night spots and discos worthy of a Waikiki Beach.

All in all, Kuta is a lively, bustling place to

The Balinese beach massage has become a popular tourist attraction in the sybaritic towns of Kuta and Sanur (above and right). Clients get a 30-minute rubdown in coconut oil, usually while being touted and watched by a madding crowd of vendors.

temple ceremonies (and formerly for their black magic), resides right there beside the upmarket tourist facilities.

Ubud, in central Bali, is the cultural heartland. The town is home to painters, woodcarvers, dancers and musicians. It attracts the more artistic and reflective visitors, including researchers, anthropologists and film-makers, who may want to do some serious work or simply gaze at the *padi*.

There is much that can be done in Ubud, from studying Balinese dancing or flute, to intellectualizing about the appeal of Bali, to soaking up the 1930s nostalgia of Walter Spies and other European artists who chose to live in this cool, lovely district in the verdant hills.

Beyond the string of art shops and galleries lining the main road is a lilting, graceful lifestyle. Art movements have been born here and the finest dances and *odalan* seem to

Singlets, shorts and psychedelia: Most Kuta togs are just too outrageous for anywhere else but Kuta Beach! The stylish, city-slick fashions in real glass-front boutiques, are further uptown. Kuta's rag-trade is a valuable spin-off from Bali's tourist industry.

The Kuta Fashion Scene

Kuta, the beach kampung *on the southwest coast, is dominated by shops. Within its rabbit warren of stalls and more up-market boutiques, cosmopolitan Kuta has developed into a flashy fashion scene for a varied foreign clientele.*

The Kuta scene is loud and sassy. It caters to two fashion seasons, the tourist influxes of December and August. At the bottom rung of the market thrives a rich trade in tops with risque slogans.

Next on the line are a riot of cheerfully colorful togs that usually prove just a bit too outrageous for anywhere but Kuta. Bright, cartoony — even dayglo — gear taunts the eye at every turn. The frivolous themes of past seasons can still be seen: naive paintings of kiddies and boats, playful patterns of ferns or dragonflies, tiger stripes, little pink squids and giant nonsense squiggles. Bali's lacey cutwork embroidery, called kerawang, *still holds its own beside rayon fun-wear, flower print froth and conventional Java-batik sundresses.*

Men have their own fashion shops too. Boutiques such as Hey Shop, Mr Bali or Indigo have sprung up carrying casual but conservative clothes that could easily be worn in international cities.

The Kuta fashion show has gone into high gear in the past three years. The new output is called "high fashion" to distinguish it from the lower 80 per cent of "flash-and-kitsch" clothes. The fanciful mood of Kuta is blended with the resort design ideas of Europeans and combined with a new awareness of quality materials. A quietly creative American textile

designer has recently wedded a wealth of old methods, such as batik tulis *(hand drawn), batik* chiap, *(stamped),* ikat *weave and silk screen, with fine new materials and contemporary motifs.*

Trendy up-market designs are now sold in over a dozen glass-fronted boutiques which are most often the brainchild of creative, long-staying foreigners. The designs marketed in the boutiques are meant for Italian, American and Japanese tastes. Arty-chic apparel has emerged under such Kuta labels as Baik Baik, Hey Shop, Libra, Ellice, Don & Donna. These are found along the noisy Legian road.

Take the tale of Baik Baik, a new success story in Kuta's retail scene. The pristine white boutique opened in April 1985, launching a colorful line-up of modish, unisex shirts in bright print designs that imitated Bali's traditional ikat *weaving. Bold, different and exclusive, they were snapped up by fashion-conscious tourists. But by September that year all impact was lost. The cloth supplier had been discovered.* Ikat *print shirts were mass-produced and selling for a fraction of the original price.*

Such tough competition makes non-stop novelty for Kuta's tourist shoppers. "Our fashions tend to be very up-to-date", says the Balinese lady behind Baik Baik. "Although the Kuta market is quite small, we have a very quick turnover of designs. The Italian and French tourists keep coming back and advising us what's popular in Europe."

It's a free-for-all fashion time for the cottage industry thriving on the sands of Kuta Beach.

thread their way through the small town.

Ubud is changing gradually, adopting various aspects of the tourist world which already pervades the southern peninsula. The painters and artisans are opening motorbike shops. Tourist dance shows are scheduled several times a week. The sarong vendors, who hawk their wares by the lotus pond, have metamorphosed into wily business folk.

Yet there remains an integrity about this cultural crossroads of arts, crafts and *orang turis*, and a consciousness about the possible effects of the tourism industry. I Made Batuan, an outspoken community leader and manager of an artists' cooperative workshop, reports that the people of Ubud are carefully preserving the traditions.

"At monthly meetings of the *banjar*, we discuss our way of life. We decide to accept or discard different things. Balinese have a solid dedication to the needs of the village above all. So we must keep the community spirit — far above individualism as known in the Western world. We must always guard against becoming too materialistic," he says.

A friendly tourist office on Ubud's main road works actively at "keeping the balance for Ubudians". The Yayasan Bina Wisata is a non-profit foundation run by volunteers whose motto is *Ubud Indah Testari*, or "a naturally preserved, beautiful Ubud".

The Bina Wisata has published an amusing, helpful map of Ubud and its environs called *The Pathfinder*. They also print the Proper Temple Dress Code poster which requests tourists attending temple festivals to wear respectful and modest attire.

Nusa Dua is the new, ultra-modern and well-planned resort village on Bali's once-deserted southeast Bukit coast, about 11 kilometers from the Ngurah Rai airport and seemingly centuries away from traditional Bali. Half a dozen luxury hotels line the sandy beachfront of the 300-hectare area. Nusa Dua is exclusive and international.

Denpasar, the historic capital city, was one of the last strongholds of the rajas before the shocking *puputan* by the court of Badung in 1906. Today Denpasar has lost all vestiges of nobility. It is an unavoidably chaotic whirlpool of motorcycles and *bemos* (three-wheeled public mini-buses), all buzzing wheel to wheel under a skyline crowded with giant movie

Soaring cloth banners called umbul-umbul *mark a place of celebration or festivity. Umbul-umbul planted all around a festival site are welcoming signposts for visiting spirits and deities, and a signal to mere mortals of a celebration.*

posters and billboards. A T-shirt says: "I rode through Denpasar and lived."

But beyond the urban, commercial cityscape is a bustling cultural life played out in schools, colleges, art academies and *banjar*. Even in urban Denpasar you will discover that vital Balinese traditions live on.

From atop Mount Agung the Balinese gods keep watch on a cremation pageant unfolding below, as it moves along the coastal

dousing event then overtakes the procession, a spontaneous addition to this most important of Balinese family rituals.

On the prestigious tourist beach, people gather with their offerings around the bull statue. The anointed body is transferred by a hundred hands into the statue's hollow back. The high priests perform a ritual blessing, then the body is sealed within and ignited with a kerosene fueled torch.

road of Sanur, from the temple to the sea, among the knot of hotels and restaurants. The community is honoring its beloved mayor, Ida Bagus Beratha, a progressive town chieftain and spiritual leader for 20 years.

A drum-and-bugle corps precedes the *gamelan* band, which is followed by a flower-bearing contingent representing every business establishment in town. Finally the big black bull sarcophagus rounds a corner soaring and swaying into view. The mammoth statue, about 10 meters tall, teeters precariously aboard its bamboo platform, which is carried on the shoulders of some 50 men looking colorful in red T-shirts. A disorderly water-

The cremation is the most important religious tradition in the intricate Balinese universe. Giant animal sarcophagi indicate caste and wealth. As bodies burn inside the bulls, souls are freed to the elements (above, right and following pages).

In the rising flames, the soul of Mayor Beratha is released, freed to the elements to return again for another life. As Covarrubias has written, "The air is heavy with the odour peculiar to cremations, which haunts one for hours after, a mixture of decaying organic mixture, sweating bodies, trampled grass, charred flesh and smoke."

Alongside the burning bull, the show captures the attention of the Sanur villagers. Elderly men of the *banjar* perform the ceremonial Baris Gede, the sacred ritual dance of warriors in honor of the departed leader. A troupe of masked character actors then entertains the captivated crowd for hours. This is the afternoon's entertainment for the villagers, and — in today's spectacle — simply another ceremony in Bali's complex tapestry.

More than just a place, Bali is an experience of color, tradition and lifestyle.

Back of the Book

This back of the book section was designed to help you push your travel experience further by informing, enlightening and entertaining you as you continue your exploration of Bali. There is a double page map of the island. Interesting Balinese traditions and legends — like that of the Tenganan horse — are revealed in *Bali Trivia*. Suggested tours take you round the galleries and shops of old Denpasar, on an arts and crafts trip through villages north of the town, on a painting tour of Ubud, and up Mount Batur. *Off the Beaten Track* tells you where to find the best shadow puppet play, the most inspired wood-carvings, which *puri* (palace) to stay in, and where to take the best photographs, amongst other interesting and unusual places to visit and things to try. *Best Bets* has a listing of the best Bali has to offer — from antiques and bird watching to bamboo furniture, books, views and fashion. *Travel Notes* gives you the travel "basics" and other advice.

Traditional woodcarving since the 1930s has seen artisans experimenting with realistic subjects taken from everyday life. This panel relief demonstrates Balinese wit, humor and sensibility and their consumate woodcarving skill. This particular work is by I Made Jojol of Batubulan.

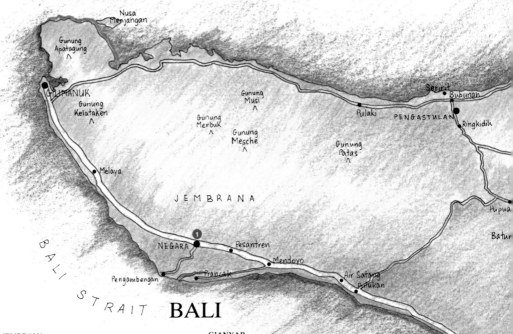

BALI

JEMBRANA
1. Negara – Western capital; site of bull races, July-Oct

BULELENG
2. Sangsit – Site of unusual temples sculptures
3. Jagaraga – Buleleng regency stronghold, lost to Dutch after fierce battles in 1849
4. Kubutambahan – Site of Pura Deuwe Karang, temple dedicated to landowners

TABANAN
5. Bedugul – Highland resort town, at 2500m, featuring recreation on Lake Bratan
6. Batukau – Site of Pura Luhur, ancestral temple dedicated to mountains and lakes
7. Tabanan – Kingdom site, 17th century; now rice belt and dance music center
8. Tanah Lot – Sea temple on an offshore islet

BADUNG
9. Sangeh – Holy Monkey Forest and 17th century temple Pura Bukit Sakti
10. Mengwi – Site of Pura Taman Ayun
11. Denpasar (Badung) – Bali's capital
12. Sanur – Beach resort hotel
13. Kuta – Popular beach town
14. Nusa Serangan – Also called Turtle Island; site of sacred temple Pura Sakenan
15. Ngurah Rai – Bali's International Airport
16. Benoa – Main Balinese harbor for pleasure and trading craft
17. Ulu Watu – An ancient and sacred sea temple
18. Nusa Dua – Ultra-modern hotel and beach resort complex

GIANYAR
19. Sukawati – Classical wayang theater village
20. Batuan – Classical music, art, dance and carvers village
21. Blahbatuh – Site of Pura Gaduh
22. Mas – Woodcarvers' village
23. Bedulu – Pre-Gajah Mada Balinese monarchy, ca. 1343
24. Pejeng – Site of the Moon of Pejeng drum, a 4th century cast-bronze masterpiece
25. Ubud – Arts and music village; tourist and student hub

BANGLI
26. Penulisan – Site of Pura Tegeh Koripan, Bali's highest situated temple
27. Gunung Batur – Much revered volcano
28. Trunyan – Bali Aga (Original Balinese) village
29. Penelokan – The place to look onto holy Mt. Batur and Lake Batur
30. Bangli – Ancient capital, ca. 1204 A.D., with sacred temple Pura Kehen

KLUNGKUNG
31. Klungkung – Noblest Balinese kingdom, last to succomb to Dutch, 1908
32. Gelgel – Ancient capital city of the Kingdom of Klungkung
33. Nusa Penida – Once a penal island for undesirable evicted from the Kingdom of Klungkung

KARANGASEM
34. Candidasa – A new tourist beach-camp
35. Tenganan – Ancient Bali Aga (Original Balinese) village
36. Tirtagangga – Magnificent rice fields and a palace built in 1947
37. Besakih – Bali's holy mother temple complex
38. Gunung Agung – The highest, holiest volcano, Bali's Navel of the world, last erupted in 1963.

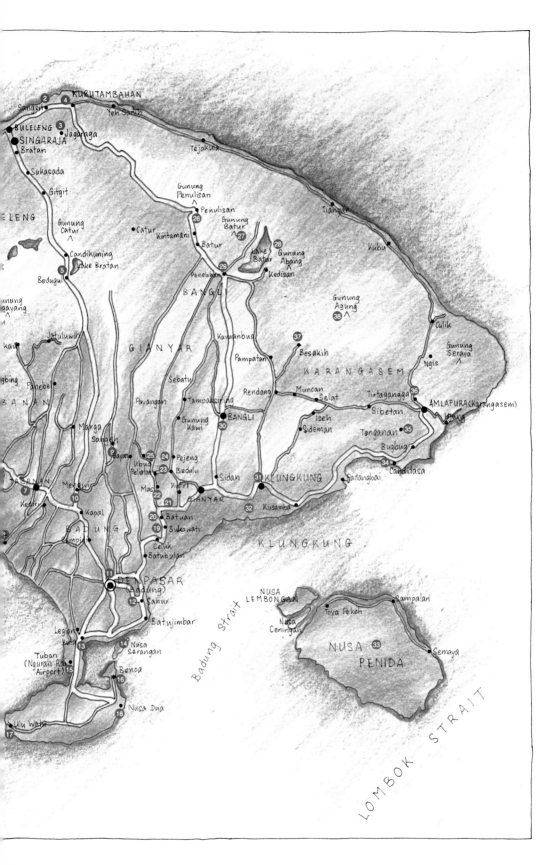

Bali Trivia

WHITE RAJAH. Mads Lange (1807–1856) was a flamboyant Danish trader who lived in Bali for 17 years, became a courageous and loyal friend to the rajas, and helped shape an interesting chapter in Balinese history. He first established a trading post in neighboring Lombok in 1834, where he was sometimes called a "White Rajah," but was eased out by dynastic rivalries and moved on to Kuta in southern Bali in 1839. There his shipping and trading enterprise flourished, and Lange fashioned himself the luxurious lifestyle of a European in the East. The energetic entrepreneur managed to deal well with the quarrelsome Balinese princes. In the 1840s, at the height of his prosperity and influence, Lange played the adept politician, acting as peacemaker between the incoming Dutch and the rajas. He died suddenly in 1856, leaving behind two wives, one Balinese and one Chinese. His only daughter, Cecilia, married a Malay prince, and two grandchildren have taken a colorful part in Malaysian royal family history.

CASTE SYSTEM. The feudalism of classical Bali had a caste system which determined one's profession, education and social position. Teachers and priests were of the *Brahman* caste and bore names beginning with "Ida Bagus" and "Ida Ayu". Warriors and soldiers constituted the *Ksatriya* caste, holding titles such as "Anak Agung", "Cokorda" or "Dewa". The merchants were of the *Wesya* caste and were titled "Gusti". These three noble castes, called the *Triwangsa*, lived in or near the palace complex. Common Balinese working outside the palace were called *jaba* (outsider) or *sudra*.

Legend had it that the *Triwangsa* had divine origins. Today the concept of caste has diminished in importance and is mostly a social affectation of the 10 per cent who make up the Balinese gentry. Recognition of caste is most evident in the use of language — there are three separate "levels" used to show respect — as well as in the manners and mores of polite society.

BUDI OF BATUAN. I Made Budi is a sensitive and witty "journalist" — with his paint brushes. He incorporates contemporary, topical characters into his canvases in the creative, syncretic tradition of Balinese culture. In 1978, Budi was sponsored on a four-month world tour to observe, and be inspired by, the diverse life of Bangkok, Hong Kong, Tokyo, Los Angeles, Las Vegas and Honolulu. After the tour, he mounted a successful solo exhibition in Hawaii. He returned to his home at Batuan, Central Bali, and named his new-born daughter Waikiki.

COCKFIGHTS. Cockfighting was officially abolished by the Indonesian government in April 1981 as part of President Suharto's policies against gambling. Bali was the exception. A cockfight is not just *allowed* at every Balinese temple festival or religious ceremony, it is *required*; blood must be spilled on the ground as an offering to the hungry forces of evil. As religious ceremonies are almost daily affairs, the tradition of cockfighting lives on. But the big public cockfights that were once regular fare in huge sports (and gambling) arenas are now a phenomenon of the past.

GAMELAN SOUNDS. The musicologist Colin McPhee described *gamelan* music as a "clear metallic sound, like the stirring of a thousand bells, delicate, confused, with a sensuous charm, a mystery that is quite overpowering". The actual word *gamelan* comes from the hammer-like mallets that produce the distinctive percussive sound, but refers to the full orchestra comprised mainly of bronze instruments. The most popular kind of *gamelan* is the *gong kebyar*, which is composed of 14 to 16 pairs of metal xylophones, two sets of gong kettles, hanging gongs, cymbals, drums, *suling* (flutes) and *rebab* (violins), and played by 25 to 30 musicians. Modern *gamelan* music is restless, flamboyant, florid, full of bold syncopations, intricate passages and shimmering cadences. It is composed of highly complex interlocking rhythmic and melodic patterns and is recognized as one of the world's most sophisticated musical forms.

ARTIST OF THE CENTURY. I Gusti Nyoman Lempad, considered "the Michelangelo of Bali", was a master artist, consummate craftsman and architect of the court of Ubud under the patronage of the influential Prince Cokorda Agung Sukawati in the 1930s, when Ubud was the center of an artistic renaissance. Lempad has been called "The greatest Balinese artist of the century." He rendered fine line drawings of Balinese life and legends, carved sacred Barong masks and designed regal stone gates for temples and palaces. Lempad lived for 112 years. He died and was cremated with full traditional honors in 1978.

BALI BELLY REMEDIES. "Bali belly" is an affliction generally caused by eating over-spiced or under-fresh foods. It attacks the best of us. The symptoms are an horribly upset stomach, maybe diarrhoea and vomiting, and a short-lived desire to end it all. Here are a few suggested remedies:

Natural cure (Courtesy: Pathfinder Map) Avoid greasy foods and take in fiber. Boil up some rice in lots of water and drink the cooking water — rich in starch, balanced for salt, sugar and vitamin B.

Traditional cure — Drink warm black tea (no sugar); take black toast (no butter). Papaya firms you up while the tummy settles down.

Chemist's cures — Norit charcoal tablets, a strong Ciba pill, Oralit to prevent dehydration, and

Lomotil to stop the runs fast. All but the last item are easily available in Bali.

KUTA SHOW-N-TELL SALON. Various artifact dealers, textile traders and island adventurers have kept up an intellectual "salon" since 1984. In a nameless corner shop, choc-a-bloc with textiles and wood sculptures, a spry Chinese art dealer plays casual host to whoever arrives after 9.30 p.m. to tell of their new buys and new adventures.

BALI BOOZE. *Tuak* is a coconut beer made from fresh juice collected from the coconut palm flower, to which yeast has been added as fermenting agent. Beware of *tuak* that has been treated with methyl alcohol as a hurry-up fermenter. *Arak* is a coconut brandy, made from *tuak* distilled down to 60 per cent alcohol. Like a western brandy, it is lovely to mix with coke or coffee. Recipe for an Ubud Toddy: *Arak* with hot orange juice and honey. *Brem* is Bali's own, favorite rice wine. The red *brem* derives from black rice; the white *brem* from glutinous rice. Try the homemade fresh white *brem* of Ubud, with a squeeze of lemon, for the nicest Bali tipple. Or try a Balinese cocktail made from one part *arak* and three parts *brem*.

GENGGONG, THE BALINESE JEW'S HARP. The "Jew's harp" is one of the simplest and most popular musical instruments in Asia. In Bali a short string attached to a delicate dry stem of sugar palm wood is "tugged" as the player blows on the vibrating wood reed. The Balinese employ a full orchestra of *genggongs* in the popular fairy tale "Frog Dance", simulating the sound of a cheerful, croaking pond full of toads.

AMULETS. Various colored semi-precious stones, usually set in huge rings, are considered "magical" by the Balinese. Worn as amulets, the stones protect the wearer against evil spirits, imbue him with personal strength and virility, deflect bullets, etc. "Magical" stones become even more powerful when worn during religious worship.

SANGHYANG. When a community is threatened by dangers thought to be caused by demons or evil spirits, the *sanghyang* dance is performed as a means of establishing contact between the gods and men. This sacred ritual clears away negative "pollution" and restores equilibrium to the village. The *sanghyang* is performed by young adolescent girls who have shown psychic aptitude. Brought into a trance by incense and group chants, they "receive" the spirits from above and dance completely possessed: entrancingly agile, incredibly together. The "Virgin Dance", performed in Bona in Central Bali for tourists, is supposed to be a shorter edition of the very sacred *sanghyang*.

BALINESE ALLURE. In 1937, chronicler Miguel Covarrubias wrote that Bali had become known to the Western world through two documentary films with a strong emphasis on sex appeal and the female body. The title of one of those films, *"Goona-goona"* (Balinese for magic) was to become, at that time, New Yorkese for sex allure.

MASKED PLAYS. The art of the masked play, *topeng*, originated in Java and was imported both as court entertainment and as ceremonial dance-drama in the temples. Classical *topeng* actors, generally three at a time, enact parts of stories taken from chronicles of the Hindu-Balinese kings. The intent of *topeng* is characterization — to show personalities first through pantomime, then through actors' conversations — which may be thoroughly esoteric and cultured, or topical, coarse and downright bawdy. There are at least 30 different *topeng* masks recognized by audiences, from refined kings to crafty courtiers and hilarious clowns.

BALINESE CALENDARS. The Balinese live by two separate but synchronized calendars. The Javanese-Balinese *wuku* or *pawukon* time system is used to determine festival dates. A year of 210 days covers 10 different weeks of one to 10 days each — all running simultaneously! The intersection of dates determines auspicious times for rituals and ceremonies. The Hindu *saka* calendar runs along a lunar cycle, and resembles more closely the western Gregorian calendar in terms of the length of a year, and religious and social activities are always planned around the full moon.

LEGEND OF THE TENGANAN HORSE. This is the story of how the Bali Aga people of Tenganan got their land. Legend has it that in the 14th century the mighty King Bedaulu lost his favorite horse and ordered a great search to be made. The men of Tenganan found the horse, or rather its corpse, in the east. As their reward, they requested possession of the land extending as far as the horse flesh could be smelt. The king sent them off with an official — a keen "smeller" — to partition the land. Long did they ride, but everywhere the air was polluted with the odor of dead flesh. The official finally left in exasperation. The Tenganan chief had carried a remnant of the dead horse under his saddle! The penis of that famous horse, now in stone, is found atop a hill near Tenganan in East Bali.

TWO BALINESE DANCERS. The late Ibu Ni Pollok, renowned as a beautiful dancer, was the wife of the Belgian painter, Le Mayeur, whom she married in 1935. She was the graceful model for dozens of canvases executed in their pavilions by the sea. Many of the paintings of her are displayed at Le Mayeur Museum in Sanur, near the Bali Beach Hotel. Ibu Pollok, once called "the epitome of idyllic Bali", said in 1980 that she saw in tourism "the means for keeping the old dances from dying

out ... without motivation it will be difficult for the arts to maintain their appeal and survive."

Cokorda Istri Ratih is today's epitome of the famous dancer. She performs regularly for shows and ceremonies in her hometown, Peliatan, for tourist functions in hotels, and for national expositions abroad. Painted and photographed by many local and foreign artists, who are attracted by her huge expressive eyes, Ratih appears on canvas, on postcards, in travel brochures and posters. This ambassadress for the arts has been dancing professionally for 15 of her 24 years and declares, "I am a dancer more by feeling and tradition, not by formal training... and I'll continue dancing forever."

RARE BIRD. The *Jala putih*, known in the West as the White Starling, is a rare and protected species, found only in Bali — and, incidentally, on the matchboxes of the Bali Hyatt Hotel.

NORTH BALI'S CHRISTIAN KING. For a brief moment in 1944, there was a Christian king or raja in Buleleng, North Bali. The Anak Agung Pantji Tistna, a direct descendant of the powerful kings of the north, was an educated and enlightened prince much dissatisfied with the sumptuous life of a royal. During the Japanese Occupation he was thrown into prison for his philosophies and there he vowed to become a Christian if he survived his ordeal. In 1944, with his father's death, Pantji became Raja. In 1946 he converted to Christianity and abdicated the royal post to a younger brother.

NUSA PENIDA. This barren isle off the southeast coast of Bali was formerly a penal colony where the Klungkung rajas dumped bad elements, criminals and couples who married out of caste. In 1979, a columnist of the *Bali Post*, Made Wijaya, called Nusa Penida "a freak side-show at the multi-ring circus of Bali's last 500 years".

KRETEKS. For many visitors, spicy clove cigarettes are the smell of Bali. The clove cigarette, called *kretek*, takes its name from the crackling sound — krrrekekekek-ek — produced when you take a long drag. The Surgeon General hasn't yet determined whether smoking cloves is harmful to your health.

GEODESIC DOME. Futurist and environmentalist Buckminster Fuller built Indonesia's first geodesic dome in Campuan, near Ubud, in the mid-seventies, right in the valley of rice padi across the road from the Tjampuhan Hotel.

NATIONALITY AND IMMORTALITY. To the traditional Balinese, Bali is a universe unto itself; religion and nationality are indivisible. If a man changes faith, he ceases to be Balinese. And conversely, no other person of another nationality can be converted to the Hindu-Bali religion and be considered Balinese. Balinese believe in reincarnation and the cycle of rebirth. But, they declare, only the Balinese have the privilege of returning to another life on their charmed island!

TOOTH-FILING. This is an initiation rite performed when an adolescent reaches adulthood, a ritual often incorporated with the wedding ceremony. The brief procedure is performed by a priest in the setting of a decorated bedstead, with bell-like *gamelan gender wayang* music as background accompaniment. The celebrant's incisor and canine teeth are filed down until they are flat and even — signifying the curtailing of the six evil qualities, including greed, anger and "earthy intoxication". Tooth-filing also removes all apparent similarity to a fanged demon. When a person finally enters the spirit world, he should not look like one of the lower animals (i.e., a Bali dog).

ODALAN-ODALAN, TEMPLE BIRTHDAYS. An *odalan* is a temple ceremony, a festive celebration commemorating the date of founding and dedication of the temple. Most of Bali's temples come to life only during such *odalan* festivities, held once a Balinese year (usually every 210 days). An *odalan* may last one, three, seven or more days. An immensely social and sometimes spectacular religious event, the temple ceremony is a vital (and highly visible) keystone in the Balinese way of life.

It has been conservatively estimated that there are well over 30,000 temples in Bali. Every village has at least three, usually more; as does every *banjar, subak*, clan, society and family. Every Balinese temple has its own *odalan*. (Juggling a few numbers of temples and anniversaries, there would be about 70 *odalans* unfolding, every day of the year!). In a week's tour around Bali, you should happen upon at least one communal village *odalan* rippling through a temple by the roadside.

VILLAGE COURTSHIP. From a village woman: "Young people's courtship is often an intangible but intense thing — no speak, no touch. It's all in a quick glance and a silent build-up of feelings... There's no room in the Balinese village society for the extended getting-to-know you, nor for the come-home-and-meet my family. The kids see each other at festivals and ceremonies. When the boy does manage to get together with the girl, she's off like a bomb: pregnant. Soon they're married."

"COCONUT WIRELESS". Gossip, news, speculation and rumors fly fast in Bali. Everyone knows where you are, what is happening in town or temple, etc. (Especially the etc.) The central exchange or nerve ganglia of this communications system is the local *warung*, the village food stand, where by standers sit around, at all hours, finding out who is doing what with whom. This morning-to-evening news report is sometimes called *Kabar angin in* Bahasa Indonesia. Translation: the "news

of the wind", meaning hearsay, rumor. Another name for it is the "coconut wireless".

A FENG SHUI TALE. The Bali Beach Hotel, erected in 1966 at the beginning of the modern tourism era, was built over an ancient cemetery ground in Sanur. The gods were displeased, everyone said. From the early days, ghostly figures and apparitions of animals "haunted" the new hotel rooms. Finally the message was received and comprehended: the villagers were to erect a temple in front of the big hotel structure! When this was accomplished — a miniscule, temple squeezed into the beachfront area — the ghosts immediately vanished and Balinese harmony was restored.

TEN GALUNGAN DAYS. The most important period in the 210-day Balinese year is the festive season beginning with Galungan and culminating with Kuningan. Galungan celebrates a legendary battle between the gods and the forces of evil. During this festive time, all the gods and the deified ancestors of each family return to earth, where they are honored and feted by their descendants.

Galungan-Kuningan is the finest time to be in Bali, as many of the most ravishing *odalans* (temple festivals) coincidentally occur all around the island. Among the most remarkable *odalans* to be experienced and enjoyed are those of:

Pura Taman Pule in Mas, Gianyar. This popular three-day social and religious affair is busy with dance and drama performances, Barong dances, trance rituals and a huge outdoor fair.

Pura Sakenan on Pulau Serangan (Turtle Island). The sacred sea temple, engulfed by boats spilling over with worshipers, is visited by two giant puppet gods, called the *Barong Landung*.

Pura Petilan in Kesiman, Denpasar. A unique ceremony called "Pengerebongan" gathers several *barongs* and many other deities in a highly charged ceremony; at one point 30 to 40 boys and men go into a trance simultaneously and stab themselves frenziedly with kris in the outer temple yard.

Pura Taman Ayun in Mengwi. This three-day *odalan* in the royal family temple features the spectacular processions of *banten tegeh* (tall fruit and flower offerings) borne by hundreds of village women walking with stately grace.

TAMPAKSIRING PALACE. "A stately pleasure dome" did President Sukarno decree in 1954 when he ordered this lavish government palace to be built overlooking one of the loveliest valleys of the island. Located high on a hill by the hallowed spring of Tirta Empul in Tampaksiring, the palace was intended as a tranquil retreat where the charismatic leader could seek respite from affairs of state. But for all its wondrous designs and landscaping, the palace acquired a very bad name. Sukarno had installed a telescope on the terrace, which he trained upon the baths below. And rumors began to circulate about other "indecorous" entertainments provided at Tampaksiring Palace.

RELATIVE TRUTH. *Bali: Sekala, Niskala* by American author Fred B. Eiseman Jr (1985) is an insightful view of the Balinese way of life. This bright yellow volume (US$26) contains a collection of essays covering all aspects of Balinese life, philosophy, arts and culture. According to Eiseman, the Balinese have a marvelous principle: The three key words are *Desa, Kala, Patra*, meaning "time, place and situation". Everything depends on these three aspects. "Truth" is relative. There are as many answers as there are people whom you ask. and this variance is sometimes frustrating.

Bali Tours

DENPASAR CULTURAL WALK. This tour takes you through the capital city's main points of cultural interest and to several modern galleries of traditional Balinese arts. Start early, around 8 a.m., with a visit to the Badung Tourist Office **(1)** on Jln Surapati. Pick up a map of Denpasar, a schedule of festivals and some up-to-date advice on events. The staff are friendly and helpful.

Cross the boulevard, passing by the national Temple of Bali (generally closed to the public) and visit the Bali Museum **(2)**, a walled complex facing the grassy open square. The museum, built in the 1920s in the form of a traditional Balinese temple and palace combined, is an architectural exhibit in itself. Three courtyards are framed by typical red brick and sandstone walls, with ornately carved gateways and wooden doors at every turn. Three museum halls display Bali's finest collections of ancient artifacts in stone and wood; traditional art forms of drama, music and weaving, and primitive tools of households and fields. Closed Mondays.

From the museum, stroll across the open field called the *Alun-Alun* — where the royal court of Badung once stood — to the three-figured bronze statue on the north end. The Puputan Monument **(3)**, erected in 1979, is a highly expressive work of Indonesian "social realism" by Jogja artist Adhi Sunarso. It pays homage to the bravery of the Balinese people who in 1906 defiantly marched to their death in *puputan* (mass ritual suicide) rather than surrender to the Dutch forces.

Continue across the open square, passing the four-faced Batara Guru statue on the crossroad. Just up Jln Veteran is the old Bali Hotel **(4)**, once the residence of colonial era visitors, before the tourism boom of the '70s. There remains a languorous air about this remnant of "Old Denpasar". Savor the nostalgia over a drink on the front terrace. Now walk along Jln Gajah Mada, the main street of the capital, named after the general who brought the Majapahit culture to Bali in 1343. Among the blocks lined with shops, offices and restaurants look out for Jln Kartini on the north side and stop in at the elegant Batik Keris store **(5)** for fine batik wear. Across the way the tape shop Toko Melati **(6)** carries the best selection of traditional Balinese gamelan music.

Cross the road and head for Denpasar's Pasar Badung fresh market **(7)**, always a bustling scene of people, goods and produce. Just across the river is the four-storey *Pasar Seni* **(8)** or art market, tightly packed with arcades of souvenir and crafts shops.

After the public market tour, walk back to the main road and then head south on Jln Thamrin, one of the busiest, most commercial roads in town. Look west between the buildings and billboards for

Denpasar Cultural Walk

a small dead-end street. Tucked inside, facing the main road, is the antique shop Arts of Asia **(9)**, one of Bali's most reputable treasure houses of art, specializing in traditional Indonesian textiles, rare ethnic jewelry and ceramics. If there is time, have a chat with art-dealer-owner Verra Darwiko. His upstairs salon and his Balinese stories are a "must" for art collectors and culturati and visitors who want to explore Balinese culture.

Finally, continue south to the next corner where stands the Puri Pemecutan **(10)**, the palace of the original Raja of Badung (Denpasar). Built to replace the former palace, destroyed with the coming of Dutch rule, the *puri* is a fine example of regal architecture. In the inner courtyard an ornately carved royal reception pavilion displays the ancient *gamelan mas*, a famous bronze instrument. In the family living compound are the traditional houses made for men and women and used for rituals. In the temple compound are many ancestral religious shrines. The descendants of the late raja run a comfortable tourist facility within the *puri*. And there is a *wayang kulit* show (shadow puppet play) every Monday and Thursday at 6 p.m. — an apt end to your cultural walk through Denpasar.

ARTS AND CRAFTS TRIP. Here is the most basic, all-in-one-day capsule tour of Bali arts for short-time visitors. If you are not driving yourself, hire a public *bemo* or minibus for the day at around US$15-25, depending on the *bemo* size and number of people. A car and driver can be arranged through any of the major hotels.

A good start is the government cooperative, Sanggraha Kriya Asta in Tohpati **(1)**, on the main road leaving Denpasar. Off the usual tour guide's art-shop route, this art center carries a full range of woodcarvings, silver, paintings, batik and *endek* — without the high-pressure sales methods used in other art shops. The center opens at 8 a.m.

JADIKAN PULUKAN DAERAH PARIWISATA

Well before 9 a.m. start the drive to Batubulan (**2**), two km. north, and catch the popular "Barong and Kris" dance show which begins at 9 a.m., at one of three venues. For Rp1,800 entrance fee, you will see an exciting, world-class Balinese dance-drama. After the show, onward to Celuk (**3**), village of silversmiths. The showrooms may be crowded, but try to visit Wayan Kantor's place, one of the better established silver galleries around. Try too Kardana's, 500 meters north off the main road. Before leaving Celuk, look for the (a misnomer!) Bali Souvenir Artshop which has a good collection of silver, ivory, Balinese folk art, curios, and artifacts.

Next stop: Mas (**4**), about two and a half km. up the road. This old village specializes in woodcarving, particularly in mask-making. For a wide selection, look for I Wayan Muka's, located east off the main road. For *topeng* masks by a master dancer-actor, see Ida Bagus Anom nearby. Finally, the Topeng Mask Exhibition, a bit north of town, is really worth exploring too.

For wooden statuary — the whole range in size, style and price — visit I Ketut Alon's gallery, located at the south end of Mas. Then, for the sheer experience, don't bypass the gallery of the most famous woodcarver, Ida Bagus Tilem, in central Mas. Here is the very best selection of Balinese woodcarvings anywhere: works of fine art show-

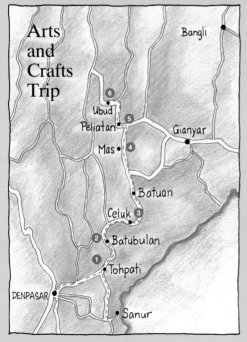

Arts
and
Crafts
Trip

cased in a sumptuous gallery attended by a polite staff. Prices are high, but just looking at a true artist's work is enjoyment enough.

Three km. north again is Peliatan (**5**), home of performing arts and many decorative arts. For elaborate fruit and flower carvings, stop by Togog's gallery on the main Peliatan road, just after you turn left at the statue of the silver dancer (marking Teges' crossing). Togog's is a delightful garden. For birds and flowers on canvas, continue about 100 meters onward to the Pengosekan Community of Artists, located on a descending side street right at the bend of the main road north. The Pengosekan workshop also applies Bali's flora and fauna to wall hangings, mirror frames, trays, boxes, trunks — lots of delightful buys for decorating.

Then, for a view of paintings in varied Balinese styles, traditional through modern, drop in at the Agung Rai Gallery, Peliatan main road. They have a good selection, although the staff can sometimes be rather pushy. By 4.00 p.m. or so, drive into Ubud (**6**) and check out the dance program on that evening. There is a good "Legong" revue on Fridays and Saturdays and a "Mahabharata" show on Tuesdays, in the public halls nearby. Buy your tickets, generally for Rp1,800–2,500.

Meanwhile, before the dance, have a meal at Cafe Lotus in the center of Ubud, by the lotus pond. Or drive on through to Murni's Warung, located down the Ubud hill by the river. Murni's has a "lovely things shop" attached, with many fine crafts, decor items and clothing. But don't get stuck browsing and buying. Be at the dance hall just after 6 p.m., when the seats start to fill up. The "Legong" dance performance — with the lively *gamelan* orchestra — will leave you buzzing for a week!

UBUD PAINTING TOUR. Taking in the entire painting scene of Ubud village can be a dizzying chore — not only because Balinese art shows such a predilection for ornament, detail and decorative splendor, but also because much of Ubud's artwork today is elaborate copyist stuff, churned out to sell to tourists. Whatever you think of the mass-produced paintings, recall the historian Hanna's judgment on Balinese art: "The incidence of great artistic skill and achievement is amazingly high, much higher, in all probability, than among any other people." Now take a leisurely, but very worthwhile, tour around the town.

Start at the Neka Museum (**1**) in Campuan, about one km. up the steep hillside on the other side of Ubud's river boundary. This is a private collection of the full range of traditional and modern Balinese paintings — a substantive, historical selection that includes works by the best-known Western artists who have chosen to settle and paint in idyllic Bali.

81

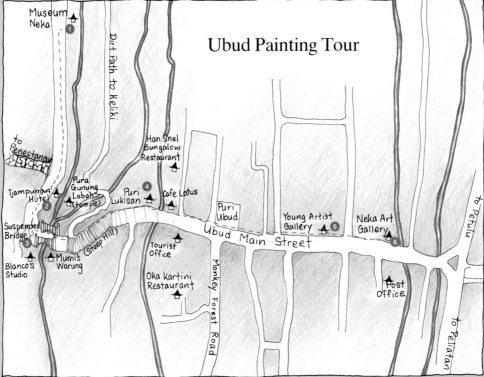

Ubud Painting Tour

Museum Neka ①

Dirt Path to Keliki

to Penestanan

Han Snel Bungalow Restaurant ☖

Pura Gunung Labah (temple)

Tjampuhan Hotel ②

Puri Lukisan ④

Cafe Lotus ☖

Puri Ubud

Young Artist Gallery ☖ ⑤

Neka Art Gallery ⑥

to Petulu

Suspended Bridge ③

(Steep Hill)

Murni's Warung ☖

Ubud Main Street

Blanco's Studio

Tourist Office

Monkey Forest Road

Oka Kartini Restaurant ☖

Post Office

to Peliatan

Walk down the hill, enjoying the view and fresh air of Campuan, before coming to the painting site (with the inspiring view) of Walter Spies, the German artist who revolutionized Balinese art in the 1930s. The Tjampuan Hotel (**2**) contains Spies' former bungalow overlooking the river. You can have a coffee and soak up the nostalgia just by gazing at the sculpted hills.

Just down the way from Tjampuan Hotel, and up a driveway, visit Spanish artist Antonio Blanco's beautiful Bali pavilions and studio (**3**). For Rp200 entrance, meet the artist in his environment. Blanco is an eccentric painter who married a Balinese dancer in the 1950s and today conjures up impressionistic artworks for the world — and inspired philosophies for his visitors. This gregarious native of Manila is a devotee of the Spanish artists Pablo Picasso and Salvador Dali.

Cross the river and walk back to the center of Ubud, to the "cultural heart" which is aptly the Museum Puri Lukisan (**4**), the painting museum of the Piti Maha society founded in 1935 by European and Ubud artists Walter Spies, I Gusti Lempad, Rudolf Bonnet and Cokorda Agung Sukawati (the

Prince of Ubud). The Pita Maha style, sometimes called "traditional", features scenes of everyday Balinese life — now painted realistically rather than stylistically — rich in colors and busy with the luxurious details of nature and village life. The best examples of Balinese "renaissance" art are gathered here in all their decorative splendor.

From the Puri Lukisan you will venture out, now more enlightened, to tour the art shops of the area. Continue your walk eastward, through Ubud town toward the Peliatan side, and stop at any of several galleries promoting the "Young Artists" (**5**). This is a vivid and vivacious, two-dimensional "naive" painting style originated by Ari Smit in Ubud in the 1960s, and repeated over the past 15 years. A Young Artists' style painting about 85 cm × 65 cm can sell for US$250. Choose with clear-eyed discretion and bargain ruthlessly.

Before 4 p.m. make it to the Neka Art Gallery (**6**) near the Peliatan boundary. This large collection runs the gamut of styles and sizes of Balinese paintings. Like the Neka Museum up north, it carries a wide selection of high quality "professional" works. Credit cards accepted.

NATURE TRIPPING OVER THE HILLS OF UBUD. There is much fine, natural scenery stretching from Ubud all the way north to Mount Batur. Here is just one basic, marvelous and fairly relaxed walk, offering a few options for trekkers.

Your starting point is Payangan (**1**), a small village about 9 km. north-west of Ubud, notable for fine rice *padi* environs and a colorful market every three days. Get there early by *bemo* (Rp150) from Ubud. (It is better to start at the higher altitude and descend — appreciate the scenery — rather than to climb uphill looking down!) At the Payangan market place, take the dirt road due east, headed for Kelusa (**2**), through a wide view of rice *padi*. About one and a half km. into the trek, at Yehtengah (**3**), you have two options.

First option: To continue east to Tegalallang (**4**). Residents will direct you to a small trail that eventually crosses a beautiful river valley to reach the main Ubud-Pujung road. From this crossroad, you can walk seven km. north to Pujung (**5**) and marvel at more rivers and *padi* views; or else you walk south, toward Petulu (**6**) (see the brown-and-white herons after 4.00 p.m.) and meander back to Ubud (three-plus km.).

Second option: from Yehtengah village, turn directly south and continue over the hillsides that roll scenically down toward Campuan. Follow the straight and well-trodden path for two hours.

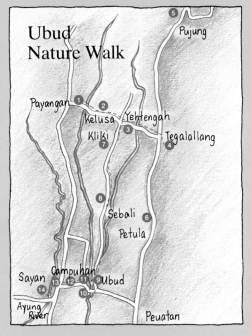

Ubud Nature Walk

Around the village of Kliki (**7**), you will notice the river running to the west. The hill then falls away into first one river valley then two. Around Sebali village (**8**) you descend a grassy meadow, a breezy corridor between two deep and steep river gorges. The hill of Campuan, called the *Bukit*, burgeons up at the fork between the waters (**9**), at the edge of Ubud, where the trail now leads you. Cross the eastern river and you emerge back on the Ubud road, just a short walk up from Murni's Warung (**10**), a perfect place for a fruit juice.

Resume the scenic walk with a trek to the west side. Cross the Campuan bridge beyond the cafe; stride 50-odd meters up the steep road. Opposite the Tjampuhan Hotel you will spot the big stone stairway (**11**), that carries you right back to the hills and *padi*. Over the steps, past the travelers' inns, follow the easy winding path through fields and small forests to Penestanan (**12**), a "Young Artists" village. A half-hour walk takes you through to the paved Sayan road (**13**). Turn south (left) walking just a short way until the big valley of *padi* fields opens into a panorama. Take the villagers' cross-country path, down to the long and winding river, Sungei Ayung (**14**). Here is a marvelous place to rest or to end a nature-walking day, basking on a huge river stone as the sun sets behind the palms and fields. From here the walk back to Ubud is about 45 minutes. Or take a *bemo*. (On another day, walk to Sangeh, the Monkey Forest,

EXPLORING MOUNT BATUR. This is one of the most interesting nature trips to do in Bali. The excursion can be done in a day, a day and a half or even longer. It covers a 4.30 a.m. sunrise over the mountain, an eerie drive over lava fields, a five-hour hike up the volcano; and a communal bath in a hot spring pool — if you do it all.

Starting point is the Mt. Batur town of Penelokan (**1**) (translated, "place to look"). Arrive there by car or public *bemo*, a two-hour ride from Denpasar via Bangli. At the look-out point on the outer edge of the 11 km. wide crater cauldron, you have a breathtaking view of the stark volcanic cone of Mt Batur, 1,717 meters high, beside the placid blue lake. (You can bask in this panorama by staying overnight at the Lakeview Homestay or Losmen Gunawan on Penelokan's cliff edge. At around 4.30 a.m., watch a tremendous sunrise from your balcony in the chill air).

From this "look-out" village, descend to the lakeside via the steep and winding road that looks closed off, but isn't. You can take a *bemo* down, or walk/drive the eight km. to Toyabungkah/Air Panas — the lakeside community that goes by varied names. The descent (500 meters) into the volcano's crater basin is exhilarating for the ever-changing

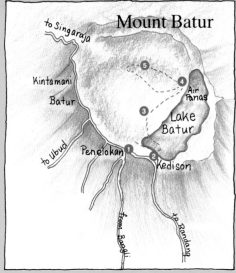

Mount Batur

vistas. At the T-crossing by the lake, where signs direct you toward the Kedisan wharf **(2)**, turn left toward the west side of the lake. Just over the rise...

Aduh! There Mount Batur's awesomeness hits you! Lava fields stretch across the horizon seemingly forever, the volcanic devastation wrought by the 1926 eruption of Batur **(3)**. Ridges and ridges of twisted and churned lava cover the once-level ground, making for an amazing roller-coaster ride along the narrow strip of asphalt that curves and rolls along the convolutions. You go up, down, left and right unpredictably, taking blind rises and curves in the lava. You arrive at Toyabungkah Art Center by the Air Panas (hot springs) **(4)**. For many, this is destination enough: to arrive and experience a sybaritic hot communal bath beside the cold lake, in the shadow of an active volcano! You can stay overnight in one of the cheap *losmens* hovering by the hot springs or at the bungalows of the Arts Center. Taste Lake Batur's unforgettable roasted fish, called *Ikan Mujair*.

Climbing Mount Batur is a steep, grueling five-hour hike, recommended only for the fit and resilient. For efficiency, contract a local guide (Rp5,000 or so). Start your Batur trek early, at 5 or 6 a.m., before the sun focuses its heat upon your struggle up the slopes from Air Panas. It is about two and a half hours' ascent at a good pace, over arid, loose, volcanic sand that slips away under foot. The last half hour to the top is the most grueling, as you clamber up at a 45 degree angle.

The climax of a Batur trek happens round the smoking crater **(5)** itself. Inside the volcano's

"mouth" the mountain falls into a dry, rocky base with steam spewing at the fissures. Outside, on a narrow edge is *you*: holding onto a crater's thin lip, standing on a slim foot ledge, and moving sideways, hand-over-hand round the crater rim for 20 minutes. The volcano's brittle crust is warm to the touch and the slope is steep...

The descent on the other side takes a bit longer. There are drink stands along the way down and a long soak in a hot spring pool to look forward to at the end of the strenuous climb.

LONG DRIVE EAST. Venture east, far from the madding crowds. This big loop drive is a full day's journey through some fine scenery, from the middle slopes of Gunung Agung, down to the sugar-white beaches of Padangbai Bay, with options to view ancient temples and palaces in between. It can be done in one 10-hour trip or you can break journey and stay overnight in the hills or by the sea. A tourist minibus with driver chartered for this route may cost around US$50–65, depending on the bus size, number of people and negotiations.

Start early, around 7.30 a.m., heading north through the arts villages. The object is to get past Batubulan village **(1)**, which gets snarled with "Barong Dance" traffic before the 9 a.m. show. Continue through Batuan and at the Sakah crossing, turn east and follow the signs for Gianyar **(2)**, capital town of Gianyar Regency. The first stop for food adventurers should be the unmarked "central market" on the main road. The best *babi guling* (roast pork) and *sate* (grilled kebab) are served in this rustic open-air setting.

Continue eastward. It is around 20 minutes to Klungkung **(3)**, once the royal capital of Bali's smallest but most noble regency. Stop at the edge of town and visit the ancient *Kerta Gosa*, the Hall of Justice, with its ceiling finely painted in the old *wayang* tradition. The best souvenir to buy here is a Bali calendar-painting — cheap, fun and comic-book quality — for under Rp2,000, if you are a good bargainer. Look for other curios in the shops.

Continue the drive to Mt. Agung. At Klungkung's main crossroad, turn north toward Besakih. A wide, smooth road gradually ascends the slopes. About 15 km. up, watch for the village of Rendang **(4)**. At this point you have two options.

You can continue due northeast and pay your respects to Bali's mother temple, Pura Besakih **(5)**, at 1000 meters altitude. (Give this visit an hour-and-a-half.) Or you can bypass the temple and turn east and take the scenic mountain drive from Rendang through the villages of Muncan **(6)**, Selat, Sibetan and Bebandem at a more leisurely pace.

The eastward road consists of a second-class, narrow asphalt strip running along the old Balinese

Long Drive East

tracks, but the view is absolutely first-class, with great panoramas of rice terraces.

A scenic option: Break the journey at Putung (**7**), the hill village with a spectacular vista of the isle of Lombok, Nusa Penida to the south, and the white beach of Padangbai below. There are quiet bungalow rooms where you can get overnight accomodation alongside the Putung Restaurant.

Descend from Putung, driving east through friendly Bebandem village (**8**) amid the *padis*. At the next crossroads — beware of a lack of signposts — veer sharply north toward Tirtagangga (**9**), the raja's water palace resort. The ascent is gentle, through wide plains of rice *padi*. At Tirtagangga, have a swim in the cool spring water pools by the giant shade trees. But be warned: the ticket man chases you for Rp500 once you are wet.

After the dip, turn back on the road and stop at Amlapura (**10**), capital town of the eastern regency of Karangasem. Drive through town to Puri Kanginan, palace of the last raja of the regency. The *puri* makes for an interesting architectural tour of a traditional royal compound furnished with eclectic taste. Visit the large veranda, called the Bale London, with its English furniture. The journey continues turning south and west (about 12 km.) toward Candi Dasa (**11**), Bali's newest beach resort village. For an ocean dip or just a splash, walk down to the beach alongside the tranquil lagoon by the main road. (You can break the trip here, take one

of the bungalows along the approach road and stay for some fine sunsets and sunrises).

Just after the Candi Dasa stopover (ideally, around 3 p.m.) continue briefly down the road to the leafy lane leading north four km. to Tenganan (**12**), a Bali Aga (original Balinese) village. Here are some of Bali's most ancient customs and unique arts. Park in the outer lot, donate your Rp200 to the village coffers and meander through the community. The people of Tenganan can be viewed weaving the rare *gringsing* (double *ikat*) cloth and writing on *lontar* (dried palm leaves). It is also worth visiting the massive rainforest tree behind.

Heading west, you will be tracing the coast of Padangbai's bay, port of call for the cruise ships. Explore the beach and headland.

Onward again, you will pass Goa Lawah (**13**) the cave full of bats, an odorous stop; then Kusamba (**14**) a salt-making village and the transport center for the eastern isles. Continue back through Klungkung and Gianyar. If it is close to 6 p.m., and if you are still game in the darkness, drive straight onward toward Ubud, Teges and Peliatan. There is always good food at the tourist restaurants and almost sure to be a Balinese dance show at 6.30 p.m. in one of the theater pavilions in the area. On a clear night here, the sky is full of stars, pathways are alive with glittering fireflies, and the only pub open late is Victor Mason's Beggar's Bush in Campuan. If Tuan Mason is on tap, buy him a drink.

Off the Beaten Track

BALI FESTIVAL OF THE ARTS. The Balinese really love their own culture and have an annual arts festival (for themselves — not tourists). From mid-June to mid-July the island goes giddy with a series of musical and dance performances unfolded on the massive open air stage and *wantilan* of the Arts Center on Jln Nusa Indah, Abian Kapas, on the south-eastern edge of Denpasar. The stages come alive with all the traditional forms of dance and drama — some of which are rarely seen today outside the remote villages. A real "heritage" treat for the Bali aficionado. For information and tickets — they go fastest for the 7-hour "Ramayana"! — call the Arts Center (tel. 22776).

SHADOW PUPPETRY. *Wayang kulit* is the ancient art of the shadow puppet play. A cast of 100 leather puppets comes to life during Balinese religious occasions. It is probably the most esoteric art form — to a tourist — but is the favorite, most jovial story-telling occasion for the villagers. The consummate artist behind the screen is called a *dalang*: he is an actor, musician, philosopher and priest. For a sample of this ancient play — albeit removed from its authentic all-night context — attend the *wayang kulit* show at Puri Pemecutan in Denpasar; Mondays and Thursdays at 6 pm. There's also a *wayang* beside the Mars Restaurant, Sanur, near the entrance to Bali Beach Hotel; shows on Tuesday, Thursday and Saturday at 6 p.m: Rp2,000 for a ticket at both locations. Bali creativity is at its best.

VISIT THE ROOT CARVER. A crowded gallery shop in Kuta (across from the Casablanca bar) full of woodcarving by the master Wayang Wetja. He is there most evenings and has been carving in both wood and ivory for 41 years.

STAY IN A PURI. Status, prestige and distinction — that's what the life of Balinese gentry is all about, even today. There is an air of politeness and gentility about the high caste descendants of Bali's old royal houses. To imbibe some of those aristocratic airs, get thee to a *puri*, an old royal palace. Several *puris* that are kept up by families allot a few rooms as visitor "homestays" for respectful guests. You meet some of the most rewarding people in a *puri*; simply walk in and ask for rooms.

The most accessible palace compound is the Puri Peliatan, just outside Ubud. Two homestays, the Puri Agung Homestay and the Semara Bawa Homestay, are set in adjoining compounds within the old palace walls; both with tranquil gardens and distinctively *sopan* (polite) Balinese families. Notice the traditional architecture; listen to the birds singing; luxuriate the puri's patriarch, Cok Parta, playing the *tingklik* (bamboo xylophone); or watch Peliatan's famous *legong* dancers hurry to and from performances. The Puri Peliatan is located under the gigantic tree along the straight Peliatan-Ubud road. The tariff is around US$3 a night.

TOYABUNGKAH ART CENTER. On the edge of Lake Batur, right by the *air panas* (hot springs) is the "futuristic, experimental art center" of Indonesian writer Takdir Alisyahbana. In the "active season" the center comes alive with *gamelan* music and dance training. There could be startling new dance choreographies, and "*gamelan* played like modern jazz"! When the artists' bungalows are unoccupied, take a room there, overlooking Lake Batur — with hot water in your rooms! You can take a two-week course in Balinese dance too. To get there, drive up to Penelokan, the lookout point over the lake, then head down to the west side of the lake, over the rugged lava fields, to the *air panas*. See the **Bali Tour** of Mount Batur.

BATUJIMBAR CERAMICS. The lovely ceramic dishes and coffee pots, seen and used in many of the best places on the island, originate from a pottery factory in Banjar Batujimbar, Sanur. From the Sanur road, just across from Hotel Taman Agung, take the road leading to the Batujimbar beach estates; turn right instead, pass the tennis courts, and you are by the gate. Ask for Brent, the New Zealand potter-designer with a fetish for Bali frogs. Or wander around the stacks of pots and plates that emerge from two giant kilns. Past all the crafts people, busily throwing and hand-building, there's a nice selection of Brent's ceramics for sale.

CALON ARANG WITH TEKTEKAN PERFORMANCE. The *Calon Arang* is a dance-drama of sacred and magical purpose revolving around the widow-witch Rangda and always performed within a temple setting to exorcise evil spirits. The Gamelan Tektekan is a pre-Hindu all-bamboo orchestra, native to the western regency of Tabanan and found today only in the ancient court of Krambitan. The haunting sound of bamboo is believed to muster magical, exorcising powers. Accompanying the sacred *Calon Arang* dance-drama, the *tektekan* makes for an unusual experience, and this can be enjoyed only in West Bali.

Every three months or so — if and when the religious calendar deems it favorable — a special Balinese "royal dinner and magical dance performance" is arranged within the old palace of Krambitan (28 km. west of Denpasar). Guests dine in the gardens in traditional, aristocratic style, then watch the *Calon Arang* dance-drama within the temple grounds. A particularly "royal" experience, if you can manage to be in the audience. Contact the agents at Bali Tours and Travel, Jln Raya Sanur 150, Tanjung Bunkak, Denpasar, (tel. 24000). And make sure they register your name for the next memorable royal soiree.

GAME FISHING. The best game fishing season stretches from June through November. In the Bali area there's Spanish and jack mackerel, white and yellowfin tuna, and skipjack to be caught out at sea and in the ocean channels. Giant trevally and Hawaiian salmon stay close to the reefs. Marlin and sailfish are rare but available also. The Bali Hyatt is the only hotel with its two fishing trollers for rent for daily fishing excursions. A fully-equipped 24-footer (for four to six persons) takes tourists fishing to Nusa Penida (half-day excursion: U.S.$250 all in). The 32-foot troller (for six to eight, U.S.$350 for a full day at sea) is, in addition, fully equipped for camping out overnight.

UBUD ARTISTS' ESTATES. For a taste of how successful Western artists live in Bali, stop in at two elegant studio-gallery-homes off the usual tourist track. Dutch artist Han Snel's Garden Restaurant is located up the graffiti-covered sidewalk across from the tourist office. This is probably the most beautiful place to stay in Ubud, amid a lovely, multi-textured garden setting with a bar overlooking a lotus pond. Snel's bungalows run from U.S.$25–35. An interesting menu includes *Canard au vin de riz vieux* (duck steamed in old rice wine) and *Susu Rangda* (coconut milk blended with rum and egg).

Antonio Blanco's showplace home is located up a steep driveway just the other side of Ubud's forked river. It costs Rp200 per entry for a glimpse of a luxurious Balinese estate. Several grand pavilions enthrone the Spanish artist and his airy gallery of contemporary paintings, mostly of his Balinese dancer-wife. Blanco is often on hand to greet visitors and talk with them engagingly.

LONTAR LIBRARY. Gedung Kirtya Historical Library, by the entry to the northern capital of Singaraja, North Bali, is a quiet, studious place containing the knowledge of Balinese ages. Here 6,000 *lontars* (palm-leaf books) are stored in a "sleep of centuries", just awaiting awakening by researchers and scholars. These organic records, some dating back to the 13th-17th centuries, repose in long slim metal or wooden boxes on crowded shelves. Ask to see the unique "book of amulets", a pictorial *lontar* describing magical formulas for *balians* ("witch doctors"). The *lontar* librarian is Nila, who may explain to you the making of these books — its done by etching calligraphic script with coal dust on dry leaves! The library is open in the morning only, except Sunday.

MEDITATION SITES. Two peaceful places to spend quiet hours … after the tourists have gone. The 11th century monastery site of Gunung Kawi, one of Bali's oldest ancient monuments, comprises 10 giant *candis* (stupas) cut into the sheer rock cliffs. Take the straight road to Tampaksiring, an easy 15 km. drive north from Ubud, and follow the signs for Gunung Kawi. Descend the long, winding stone stairway that goes deep down into a river valley totally sculpted with rice terraces.

Another sublime place is the garden temple of Taman Ayun, built by the royal family of Mengwi in 1627. This temple was built as a place to worship royal ancestors, whose spirits are honored in a special shrine within the sacred grounds. There is a great sense of calm and peace among the towering, multi-roofed shrines and the carp-filled moat. Mengwi is located about 17 km. northwest from Denpasar, an easy drive in the direction of Sangeh Monkey Forest. To stay in the temple overnight, contact the family-trustee and keeper, Anak Agung Gde Tisna Mayun, a friendly aristocrat who "holds court" in the open pavilion in the central courtyard of tranquil Taman Ayun temple.

CHASE A BABI GULING. The Balinese love their roast pig straight off the spit, dripping with fat, golden-skinned, unceremoniously hauled in and carved at the table by the *ibu* (matron) of the food stand. A plateful costs an average of Rp750.

In Denpasar two places serve good *babi guling*: the "Bali Guling Gianyar" Restaurant on Gianyar Street; and the Rebo Restaurant (and several others nearby) on Jln Diponogoro, Sesaten area, on the road out toward Benoa. In Gianyar town itself, where the "secret recipe" of *babi guling* originated, find the tastiest roast pig right along the road: drive 27 km. east from the capital; at Gianyar town look left for the open but unmarked market place, and follow the beguiling aromas.

BEDUGUL-SINGARAJA-LOVINA. From the tourist hubs of the south, head north toward Singaraja, capital of Buleleng Regency. It is a long (80 km. from Denpasar) but exhilarating drive, full of sharp, winding curves, mountain panoramas, and the fresh clean air of the Bali highlands.

Stop by the new resort town of Bedugul for lunch, or overnight at one of the two large hotels in town. Stroll over to Lake Bratan for temple-gazing at the serene Pura Ulu Danu on the lake or have a try at water-skiing or windsurfing. Or alternatively wander among the fruit orchards and vegetables gardens around Bedugul.

Singaraja, on the northern coast, is a sprawling modern town with a Dutch-cosmopolitan feel and some wild and expressive temple carvings. Drive west about 15 km. and stay at Lovina Beach Village. Here 15–20 *losmens* (inns) are strung spaciously along the quiet black-sand beach. Watch the sunsets by evening …

By day drive far west to Pulaki Bay, or east (15 km. past Singaraja) to Yeh Sanih for idyllic seaside experiences.

PANDANUS FIGHTS IN TENGANAN. In the middle of the year, in June or July, the men of Tenganan, the Bali Aga (Original Balinese) Village of East Bali, fight till the blood flows. Stripped to the waist, and armed with bundles of *pandan* fronds — thorns facing outward — and circular bamboo shields, pairs of "gladiators" spar in quick, lightning matches. The object is to get in close and scratch the opponent's exposed body. Called *Perang Pandan*, or *Mageret*, this blood-shedding ceremony is part of the annual Usaba Sambah festival. To reach Tenganan Village from Denpasar, drive some 70 km. east, toward the capital town of Amlapura. Along the large coastal bay, one kilometer before reaching Candi Dasa beach town, take the leafy road spiraling four kilometers uphill to the ancient but neatly walled village of Tenganan. Other unusual cultural items to be witnessed here in the most conservative village of Bali are the ancient orchestra, the *gamelan selunding*, which plays low and slow; the rare, double *ikat* cloth called *gringsing*, woven only in Tenganan; and the production of *lontar*, the traditional palm-leaf books.

SCUBA AND SNORKEL. Bali's underwater paradise is only just now revealing itself to goggle-eyed Westerners. Diving is possible off Sanur Beach or Nusa Dua where scuba-training is offered, but experienced sports divers would do well to head for the main diving sites around the islands. Ask about excursions at Bali's PADI resort, c/o Hotel Bualu Nusa Dua (tel. 71310). Suggested destination:

Padangbai, 90 km. northeast of Sanur — picturesque white-sand bay surrounded by cliffs, with impressive dives over full coral growth. Ideal depth are from three to 20 meters.

Tulamben, 100 km. northeast of Sanur — a wreck dive on the US cargo ship *Liberty*, sunk during the Second World War (at 30 meters depth).

Singaraja, 80 km. north of Sanur — calm waters just offshore for leisurely snorkeling; ideal for scuba-beginners. Also try Lovina and Gondol.

Pulau Menjangan, 120 km. northwest of Sanur, plus a 10-minute boat ride — magnificent diving waters full of diverse sea life and marine gardens; best vistas for underwater photography.

Nusa Lembongan (Bali's "sister" isle), 20 km. east of Sanur (two hours by motorboat) fine diving over white sands and marine gardens.

MOUNT BATUKAU AND THE THREE TEMPLES TOUR. This is a long tour up a western mountain and down to the sea. Start early, driving toward Tabanan, capital of the southwestern rice belt. Three km. before town, stop by the new Museum Subak, on a hillside overlooking Kediri. The farmers' museum displays tools used in the rice fields and traditional home implements. Proceed through Tabanan and head north to Mt Batukau, along the long straight road through rolling terrain of rice fields. About 20 km. up, follow signs to Wongaya Gede, a village below Pura Luhur, the old state temple dedicated to the spirits of mountains and lakes. Park and amble about one km. up through the rainforest of Mt Batukau (2,276 meters), known as the "coconut shell mountain".

From Pura Luhur, drive eastward to the tiny upland village of Jatiluih where you have a truly marvelous view of the mountain running down to the southern sea. Continue on a rather serpentine road to the junction town of Pacung, where you can enjoy a very tasty luncheon at the marketplace. Next, turn south on the highway to Mengwi. Before 2 p.m., visit the Museum Manusa Yadnya of Mengwi, depicting Bali's "human being ceremonies" in photos, statuary and palm-leaf offerings. Just across the way, stroll through Pura Taman Ayun, the royal family temple (built in 1637) surrounded by gardens and moats. The Mengwi people are very proud of their temple and lavish great attention on Taman Ayun at festival time. At 3.30 p.m. leave Mengwi and drive directly south (one hour) for Tanah Lot on the coast, to view a dramatic sunset at this famous temple.

CANDI DASA SUNSET. Beach town in East Bali. Candi Dasa lies about 70 km. east from Denpasar, on the bay side of Tenganan village, right along the coastal highway. Be there at 4.30 p.m., head down to the fine, white sand beach and sit on the outer wall. Bask in a wide, engulfing pink sunset then wander into one of the small cafes along the main road and dine on fresh fish for just Rp750.

BULL-RACES OUT WEST. After the rice harvests, usually between July and November, the farmers of Negara, the capital of the eastern regency of Jembrana, bring out the beasts of burden to race. Bulls with painted horns are teamed up to pull heavy carts — with a jockey-driver. Up to 100 teams go thundering down a two km. dirt track at speeds of 50 mph! Negara lies 95 km. west of the capital.

UBUD. Here are four diverse and interesting aspects of Ubud: 1. The Bali Hash House Harriers Club meets in the Beggar's Bush Pub on Campuan road, just across the river. They run cross-country around Bali every Monday afternoon at 4 p.m. 2. The Cafe Lotus on the main road serves interesting cuisine — home-made breads and pasta, fine salads, and thick vegetable soups. 3. The Monkey Forest Hideaway, on the edge of Ubud's small monkey forest, is the coziest new *losmen* around, loaded with rustic charm and riverside scenery. 4. Purpa's Art Gallery, the big white "department store" by the padi along Monkey Forest Road, carries textiles, paintings, silver and postcards.

Bali Best Bets

ANTIQUES AND ARTIFACTS. The Arts of Asia Gallery, Jln Thamrin 27–37, Block C5 Denpasar (tel. 23350) has the finest selection of rare Indonesian textiles, ethnic jewellery, ceramics. Borneo Art Shop, Jln Legian, Kuta (tel. 51834) has woodcarvings, silver, ivory and Indonesian textiles. Z. Baharuddin, Jln Bakung Sari, Kuta, has textiles, traditional Indonesian art, curios and antiques.

BAMBOO FURNITURE. Handsome bamboo seating sets upholstered with modern *ikat* weaves or batik from Linda and Amir's Showroom, 19 Padang Galak, on Sanur bypass road.

BAKERIES. For good smells, pies and breads fresh from the oven try Gelael Supermarket and Bakery, Jln Imam Bonjol, Kuta. Also, Yudit's Place, Jln Legian, Legian, near the *bemo* corner. Do get there early while the bread is warm.

BALINESE FOOD. Although it is not easily available and must be ordered at least 24 hours in advance (see page 50), fine Balinese cuisine can be prepared with upmarket flair by the Tandjung Sari Hotel, the Kulkul Restaurant and the Bali Hyatt Hotel, all in Sanur. In Kuta, try Prawita Garden Restaurant, Jln Legian. The international menu includes special Balinese fare such as *Sate Lilit, Sate Penyu, Sop Kambing*. In Ubud, try *Bebek Betutu* (smoked duck) cooked in authentic Peliatan style. At Murni's Restaurant, near the river, you can get a full Balinese *Bebek* dinner for about Rp7,000 for two. Okawati's Restaurant off Monkey Forest Road has tasty duck with all the trimmings for Rp6,000. At Ubud Restaurant, Monkey Forest Road, there is a wide variety of Balinese cuisine served in a rice *padi* setting. Cafe Lotus on the main Ubud road is the only place with four portions of *Bebek* readily available daily; Rp3,000 for a full meal.

BATHS. Hot bath at Air Panas, Toya Bungkah, on the very edge of cool Lake Batur. Men and women soak together in the knee-deep outdoor pool. Bring a towel, no charge. Cold swim at the pools of the Water Palace of Tirtagganga north of Karangasem, East Bali. Rp500 for a quick, clear dip. This springwater swim is most refreshing.

BIRD WATCHING. The brown and white herons of Petulu village, two km. east of Ubud, come home to roost at 4.30 p.m. every afternoon. Turn west off Petulu main road by the umbrella maker's shop, and bring a good telephoto lens for some fine feathered photos. A unique Ubudian experience.

BOOKS. Best general reads: *Island of Bali* by Miguel Covarrubias (1937) is a kind of a socio-cultural "bible". *Tale of Bali* by Vicki Baum (1937) is a novel based in Sanur and Badung before the 1906 *puputan*. *The Balinese* by Hugh Mabbett (1985) is an introduction to Bali today. *Bali: Niskala, Sekala* by Fred Eiseman, (1985), has comprehensive essays on aspects of Balinese culture. *Night of Purnama* by Anna Mathews (1965) is an autobiographical story of the 1963 eruption of Mount Agung. Specialized books are: *Bali Profile* by Willard Hanna (1985), an immensely readable history. *Split Gate to Heaven* by Rudolf Mrazak (1985) is a luxurious book on Balinese art and culture. *Paon Bali*, produced by the Bali Hyatt, (1984) is a handy introduction to Balinese cooking. Book of Indonesian phrases: *Speak Indonesian* by John Barker, (1985) has basic Bahasa Indonesian for tourists and travelers.

BOOKSTORE. For up-to-date English newspapers, and a reasonably good selection of books on Balinese subjects, visit Guna Agung on Jln Diponegoro, by the river in Denpasar.

CARVED NAME PLATE. Impress your colleagues with your name and title hand-carved on an ebony desk plaque. Rp10,000 to 15,000 in handicraft shops everywhere. Cost depends on the intricacy of carving and amount of gilt trim.

CHINESE FOOD. In Sanur, try Si Pino Restaurant, Jln Raya Sanur, near the Bali Beach Hotel. A more expensive treat can be had at Telaga Naga Restaurant near the Bali Hyatt Hotel. In Kuta, the Bali Indah on Jalan Pantai serves up Chinese cuisine. In Denpasar, Atoom Baru Restaurant on Jln Gajah Mada. For gourmets, Feng Shen Restaurant, Kumbasari Center, Jln Gajah Mada, where food is authentic, delicious and cheap.

CELEBRITY GAZING. The best place to catch sight of rock and movie stars and other beautiful people traveling incognito is the Tandjung Sari Hotel flanking the beach at Sanur.

CURRIES. Goa Restaurant, Legian Road, Legian. Warung Kopi, Jln Legian, Legian, has three tasty Sri Lankan curries on its menu. Sonia's Curry House on the bypass road, Sanur, is quiet but good.

DISCOS. In Sanur: Number One Club, in a stylish Balinese pavilion, attracts the young tourist set; Sub'ec Disco has a hall of mirrors, loud music and a local businessmen clientele; Matahari, a Juliana's club at the Bali Hyatt, is upmarket, with Rp4,500 entrance fee. In Kuta and Legian: Peanuts is strictly casual, singlets and thongs allowed; Cheater's Makan Club is a modern high-tech disco with a sound and light show, no singlets and thongs allowed; The Double-Six Restaurant is the Friday night club of Europeans and fashion folk; Gado-Gado pulls a trendy, mixed crowd of Kuta people.

EAST-WEST CUISINE. Made's Warung, Jln Pantai, Kuta, has a steady high standard of Indonesian and western food. Atmosphere is lively, and bohemian. Good *rijstaffel* on Saturdays. Also, grilled squid, *nasi campur* and more. To top it all, the best jazz-rock background music in town.

EUROPEAN CUISINE. Fine French cooking at Topi Kapi in Legian, around Rum Jungle Road. Patio Restaurant, in the vicinity of Jln Padma, Legian, has good continental food, great cakes and Italian dishes. For good pasta, try Trattoria da Marco, Jln Raya Sanur, Sanur; Kuda Kayu Italian Restaurant, Jln Legian, Kuta; and Cafe Lotus, located on the main road in Ubud.

FACIAL. A luxurious traditional Indonesian facial treatment with natural Javanese cosmetics at the beauty shop of Bali Hyatt, Sanur, for Rp12,000; or at Sari Ayu or Ratu Ayu, two leading beauty salons in Denpasar, for around Rp3,500.

FASHION PARADE. Drink capuccino and have a piece of rich rum chocolate cake at Made's Warung, Kuta. Lots of European artists, traders and rag-trade folk. The outfits and the atmosphere are zany and zingy. A *jeunesse d'orée* set nightly.

FRESH FISH. For the best fresh fish for your rupiah, try Bali Indah Restaurant, Jln Pantai, Kuta. Lobis King of Seafood, Jln Legian, is best value for fish and chips. Made's Warung, Jln Pantai, Kuta has tunafish served with spicy Balinese sauce. Rumah Makan Sadarasa, Jln Sanur Beach, Sanur, has little atmosphere but great grilled fish. Try Mak Beng's Warung at the end of Hotel Bali Beach road.

FROG DANCE SOIREE. An entertaining and delicious Balinese dinner-and-dance-show can be arranged at the rustic-elegant Kulkul Restaurant, Jln Hyatt, Sanur. Kulkul offers a choice of Balinese dinners for minimum eight persons: *Bebek Betutu* (smoked duck) or *Babi Guling* (roast piglet), with *sate*, *ikan pepes*, and *brem* on the side. Make arrangements well in advance (tel. 8038).

GAMELAN ON CASSETTE. The dizzying gamut of *gamelan* music and other Indonesian sounds from ancient Balinese to ultra bubblegum at Toko Melati, Jln Kartini 17 off Gajah Mada Road, Denpasar (tel. 2092). Bargain prices too.

GARDEN RESTAURANT. The well-known Poppies Restaurant on Poppies Lane in Kuta has an intimate ambiance and lovely natural setting. A family favorite. The international menu includes steak, *sate* and grilled fish. Prices are reasonable.

GOLF. In the highlands of Bedugul up north, Bali Handara Hotel and Golf Club has reputedly the best golf course in Southeast Asia. Closer to the sea, at the Bali Beach Hotel, Sanur, golf is played alongside the tallest building on the island.

ICE CREAM. At the Tandjung Sari Bungalows try the coconut ice cream. At the Bali Hyatt coffeeshop have one of the homemade ice cream flavors made from fruits in season, such as soursop or durian. At Trattoria da Marco, Jln Raya Sanur, have a hefty helping of chocolate ice cream.

JOGGING TRAIL. Bali Hyatt in Sanur has a 500 meter jogging path through the hotel's exotically landscaped gardens. Running partners and timers can be hired from the hotel.

KECAK DANCE. Visitors to Bali should not miss this dramatic dance spectacle, derived from ancient trance ceremonies, where 100 men vigorously chant like monkeys. The Arts Center, Jln Nusa Indah, Denpasar, has daily performances from 6 to 7 p.m. Daily shows at the same hour are also held at Pura Ayodya in Tanjung Bungkak under the big tree on the way to Sanur. Admission to both is about Rp1,800. Best bet for Balinese showmanship.

LEGONG SOIREE. On some Saturday nights the Tandjung Sari Hotel in Sanur holds a scintillating Balinese evening with palm leaf buntings and *gamelan* music fanned by the ocean breezes. Highlight is the *legong*, dance performed by Bali's finest dance troops — from the ASTI Academy, the Saba Village or the Peliatan Village groups. The dance is followed by Indonesian *rijstaffel* buffet with a good selection of Balinese cuisine. Inquire ahead (tel. 8441). For connoisseurs of the *legong*.

MAP. The Pathfinder Map of Ubud and environs is an unusual fold-out map which introduces some great rural walks and has an off-beat introduction to Balinese culture, society, food, medicines, habits and tastes. Map costs Rp1,500 at the tourist office on Ubud's main road, more expensive elsewhere.

MASSAGE. Many village women who have learned basic massage can be found along Sanur Beach, especially between Santrian and Gazebo Hotels. They give a good rubdown under the coconut palms for Rp2,500 and up. Or try and locate Ibu Kasur, a matron from Madura living in the *Sindhu* neighborhood of Sanur. She specializes in females. Sanur's most professional masseur is the blind Ketut Landra, who has had 15 years of experience. He has a one-room clinic with a sign hanging outside: Dirgahayu, on Jalan Hyatt in Sanur. Landra charges Rp4,000 to 10,000 an hour, depending on the client and location. This can be arranged by your hotel.

MEXICAN FOOD. Good Mexican-American fare can be had at TJ's Restaurant on Poppies Lane, Kuta, along the long diagonal pathway leading to the beach. (Tacos, enchiladas, tortillas and nachos).

MUSIC CASSETTES. Mahogany Tape Shop on Jln Legian, Kuta, opposite Prawita Restaurant, has a great range of the latest rock and jazz sounds at a fixed price of Rp1,750. Good listening, quick service, and happy impromptu dancing.

NASI CAMPUR. This very traditional Balinese dish of rice piled high with several dishes of the day can be had at the roadside Warung Teges right by the Peliatan marker-stone. The *ibu* (matron) serves only *nasi campur* and you take whatever she has cooked that day. Up to 10 choices of dishes.

PARA-SAILING. See the sandy coast of Sanur from high above. A motor boat pulls parachute and passenger round the lagoon for about U.S.$10 for an exhilarating ride. You will find the para-sailors and boat on Sanur beach, just alongside the Bali Hyatt water-sports area.

PAINTED BUS. The Tandjung Sari Hotel's bus is covered with naive "Young Artists'" paintings. It runs a shuttle service to and from the airport by special arrangement with the hotel.

SANUR COCKTAILS. Try Ronny's Restaurant, Sanur Beach Hotel, for elegant mixed drinks in new classy surroundings. At the Blue Diamond Restaurant, Jln Hyatt, you can have a good Singapore Sling in a slightly dowdy, 1950s atmosphere.

SCUBA DIVING PACKAGE TOURS. The Gloria Maris Club, Jln Raya Kuta, 10 km. Kuta (500 meters south toward the airport), offers accommodation, airport transfers, transport to four diving locations around Bali: *Padangbai Bay,* on the east coast; *Tulamben* on the northeast coast — dive in the wreck of the American ship, *Liberty* ; *Menjangan Island,* northwest of Bali; and *Kambing Island,* 16 km. off the northeast coast. Diving packages for groups or individuals available. Daily or weekend rates average U.S.$50 to $60 a day. (tel. 23730).

SCUBA CLASSES IN BALI. The most complete scuba teaching facility on Bali is at the Hotel Bualu, Nusa Dua (tel. 71310). Take a six-day diving course conducted by certified instructors for around U.S.$150. Or join one of the hotel's picnic and diving excursions arranged to nine underwater destinations; favorites are Padangbai Bay and Pulau Menjangan in the northwest.

SAILING AND SNORKELING. Take one of the colorful *jukung* sailboats lining Sanur beach to snorkeling sites near Turtle Island. One to two passengers per boat for Rp8,000 to 10,000 an hour, depending on time, client and season. Negotiate on the beach. Snorkeling equipment is provided.

SPORTS-ORIENTED HOTEL. The Hotel Bualu in Nusa Dua packages total, sportsy vacations for guests. Facilities — and instructors — for tennis, horseback-riding, windsurfing, surfing, sailing and snorkeling come free-of-charge with your stay. Scuba-diving courses and "miniclub" facilities for the kids are available at very reasonable charges.

SUNSET. The sacred temple of Tanah Lot on the west coast offers a fabulous sunset view. The temple is suspended on a rock about 200 meters offshore.

TEXTILES AND WEAVINGS. The long-established AAA shop on Jln Veteran, Denpasar, near the Nitour office, has *endek* (Balinese *ikat*) and good Balinese sarongs. Large selection, reasonable prices and an old Denpasar atmosphere. In Kuta, visit Alex's shop on Jln Legian, opposite Fatty's Restaurant. Alex sits amidst a wide array of textiles, genuine *ikat*, batik sarongs and a large collection of *ajat*, woven tote bags from Kalimantan. Prices are fixed so don't try bargaining.

UBUD FOOD. The Cafe Lotus has freshly made pasta and cakes. Murni's Restaurant has *nasi campur*, spicy Balinese chicken and the *bebek* or smoked duck dinner. The Ubud Restaurant on Monkey Forest Road has *sate lilit*.

VIDEO FILMS ON BALI. Several rare documentary films on Bali are available for members' and friends' viewing in the Rumours Lounge of Tandjung Sari Hotel, Sanur. Best films: *The Eleven Powers* (1980) by Larry Gartenstein covers the great Eka Dasa Rudra ceremony of 1979 and is narrated by Orson Welles. *Lempad of Bali* (1980) by Lorne Blair and John Darling is about the remarkable artist I Gusti Lempad, whose century-long life spanned Bali's modern transformation.

VIEWS. For the sheer spectacle of mountains, rice terraces, seas and winding rivers, here are some favorite scenic drives and vantage points:

Putung in Karangasem, on the high and winding road about an hour north and east from Klungkung. This breezy, strategic spot on a high cliff overlooks the perfect white sands of Padangbai Bay, the sea, Nusa Penida and Lombok Island in the distance.

Pujung-Sebatu, about 10 km. east of Ubud. A very accessible photo-site for picturesque rice terraces spilling down the river gorges.

Demulih, Bangli, a well-known vantage spot just one km. west of Bangli town. Park by the road and hike just 100 meters up the hill on the edge of town for a stunning panoramic view of Mt. Agung, the eastern sea and Lombok Island beyond.

Jatiluih, Mt. Batukau, 5 km. east of the ancient temple of Pura Luhur, along a narrow "road" some 25 km. north of Tabanan, central-west Bali. This tiny village, 850 meters up, affords a view of the landscape of the whole of south Bali, stretching towards the forests of the west.

Sayan, three km. west of Ubud. Right off the Sayan road, by the sign of the Putra Painter Group of Young Artists, a footpath leads to the cliff's edge, to a special spot overlooking a panorama of terraces and the beautiful, winding Agung River. A paradise for lovers and photographers.

WINE. Kawan Jaya Botol Shop, Jln Pantai, Kuta. Good French Blanc de Blanc for around Rp7,500. Beaujolais for around Rp9,500.

WOODCARVING. A fun mixture of carved and painted masks, sculptures, frogs, frames, cherubs and mermaids can be found at the nameless, barn-like shop just across the road from the Puri Lukisan museum in Ubud. You will recognize it by the hairy Rangda heads on the door.

Travel Notes

Land and People

Bali, one of the smaller islands of the Indonesian archipelago, is located at 115° east longitude and 8° south latitude, just below the equator. It lies three km. off the eastern coast of Java and is the first of the Lesser Sunda islands. Bali has a land area of 5,632 square km. A dramatic chain of mountain volcanoes runs clear across the northern length of the island. In the east towers Gunung Agung at 3,142 meters, revered as the "mother mountain". On the fertile southern slopes of the mountains, between the two major rivers, the Pakrisan and the Petulu, the most ancient culture of Bali was born.

Bali is the second most densely populated of the 27 provinces of the Republic of Indonesia. The capital is Denpasar. The island's 2.6 million population is divided among the eight regencies or counties: Badung, Bangli, Gianyar, Jembrana, Karangasem, Klungkung and Tabanan. The Balinese made their living firstly by agriculture — with rice, copra, coffee and tobacco as the main crops — and secondly by tourism. The developing tourist industry generates income through the hotel, transport and peripheral trades as well as through the sale of Balinese crafts such as woodcarving, silverwork and both schools of painting.

Bali-Hinduism, properly called Hindu Dharma, is the religion of 90 per cent of the Balinese. Basically they worship one supreme God, Sanghyang Widi Wasa, who is manifested primarily in the Hindu trinity of Brahma, Siva and Vishnu — as well as in a huge pantheon of everyday nature spirits and other minor deities. Bali-Hinduism, also called Balinism, is essentially an animist faith with an overlay of Indian Hindu practices. Their religious practice involves the cults of ancestor worship, sacrifices of blood, Brahmanic juggling of mystic words and tantric symbols, and the all-important cremation of the dead to release the spirit to participate again in the karmic cycle of reincarnation.

How to Get There

By air:

Garuda Airlines flies international visitors from Indonesia's capital city of Jakarta several times daily for about U.S.$90 one way. Several airlines fly directly to Bali, bypassing Jakarta, from their national capitals. These included — at the end of 1986 — Singapore Airlines, Malaysian Airlines, Qantas and Cathay Pacific.

By sea:

Cruise ships such as the *Island Explorer* call at Padangbai, the eastern port. This is generally a brief stopover rather than a conventional visit to Bali.

By Road and Rail:

Denpasar, capital of Bali, lies 1000 km. from Jakarta, the capital of Indonesia on Java Island. First-class air-conditioned coaches to Bali are operated by two companies — PT Jawa Indah and PT Beautiful Continental. The Jakarta-Denpasar bus leaves daily, the journey takes about three days and the cost is around U.S.$26.

One of the most comfortable and scenic ways to arrive in Bali is to go overland from Java by train, bus and ferry. The first-class Bima Express or Mutiara Express leave Jakarta's Kota station around 4 p.m. daily, and arrive in Surabaya, East Java, at 8.30 the next morning; about U.S.$19. From Surabaya, another train to Banyuwangi connects to a bus ride into Denpasar or a coach goes all the way from Surabaya to Bali. Both ways take about 10 hours. Cost: about U.S.$3.50 one way.

Airport

The airport tax of Rp6,000 per person is levied on all passengers on international flights out of Bali. Domestic airport taxes vary from Rp 800 to Rp 2,500. A taxi service operates from Ngurah Rai International Airport, 12 km. southwest of Denpasar. The prices for destinations are listed at the taxi kiosk just outside of the arrival building, where the taxi fare must be prepaid. It costs about Rp7,800 from the airport to Sanur or Nusa Dua.

Bargaining

Bargaining is a major part of a tourist's experience of Bali. Goods and services are not the same price everywhere. Price depends on the time, place and situation of both the vendor and the potential customer. Treat bargaining as a friendly game and as a means of contact with the Balinese. Generally, prices will decrease in direct proportion to the time spent in Bali, your experience and "goodwill".

Camping

There is only one facility catering to scouts and camping lovers. The old Boy Scouts camp in Blahkiuh, 500 meters off the main road going up toward Sangeh Monkey Forest, has ample and scenic camping grounds, public baths and toilets by the lotus ponds, plus a kitchen area and five basic cottages on the upper hillside. Ask for permission at the Anak Agung Mayun's residence just across the main road going to Blahkiuh.

Charter Transport

Transport-for-tourists is a growth industry. Mini-buses and taxis waiting outside the large hotels, or public *bemos* plying the roads, can be privately "chartered" for short inter-city runs (say, Sanur to

ATTENTION PLEASE

1. DEAR GUEST YOUR COOPERATION IS REQUESTED IN INSURING QUIET AFTER 10 PM.
2. NO FOOD CAN BE ORDERED AFTER 8 PM.
3. CHECK OUT TIME BEFORE 12 MD.
4. THE ELECTRICITY WILL BE TURNED OFF AT 12 PM. WE WILL SUBSTITUTE WITH KEROSENE LAMPS.

Kuta) or for all-day trips (say, Sanur to Besakih and back). Everything depends on your negotiations with the vehicle driver. Prices are determined by the size and type of transport, the distance to be traveled, the time required and the skill of the negotiator. A public *bemo* chartered from Sanur to Kuta costs around Rp 3000 one way. A roomy, comfy mini-bus chartered for a standard day-trip to the villages (usually 70 km. away) costs Rp40,000 to 50,000. See page 96 for more guidelines.

Clothing

Bali is generally informal in the tourist towns of Kuta, Sanur and Nusa Dua, but conservative and "polite" in the villages. Brief attire — meaning shorts and skimpy tops — is frowned upon except by the sea or hotel pool. Casual, cool, but covered-up clothing is most suitable. A warm sweater or jacket is recommended for trips into the mountains.

Communications

The central Post Office is in the new City Civic center of Renon on the Sanur-Denpasar bypass road, Jalan Puputan Raya. It is open from 8 a.m. to 2 p.m., Monday to Thursday; 8 a.m. to 11 a.m. on Friday; and 8 a.m. to 1 p.m. on Saturday. There are branch offices with longer opening hours in the first class hotels and among the villages.

The Telephone, Telex and Telegram Office is located just behind the Badung Tourism Office on Jln Surapati in Denpasar. Bali is linked via satellite to all major countries in the world. But international connections may take time and there are no reverse-charge facilities to most Asean countries. The automatic International Subscriber Dialling system (IDDI), whereby no exchange operator is required, has recently been installed at the telephone station in Kuta, near the airport.

Climate

Bali has two seasons: the dry season from April to September, with hot days and cool evenings; and a wet season from October to March, with heavy tropical showers alternating with clear sunshine. Average temperatures vary from 28°C to 30°C with a temperature drop of 10° in the mountain regions. The most pleasant months to plan your stay are between May and September.

Consulates

Australian: Tanjung Bungkak, Denpasar; tel 25997 & 25998.
Japanese: Tanjung Bungkak, Denpasar; tel 25611.
American: Jln Segara, Sanur; tel 8478.
Italian: Jln Padanggalak, Sanur; tel 8372.
Swedish: Jln Segara, Sanur; tel 8231 & 8407.

Customs and Visas

As of April 1, 1983, visas were waived for nationals of 26 countries for a visit of no more than two months. This tourist pass is not extendable. Regulations prohibit the importation of weapons, narcotics and pornography. A maximum of two liters of alcohol, 200 cigarettes, 50 cigars or 100 grams of tobacco and a reasonable amount of perfume may be imported into the country.

Dance and Drama

Visitors with a short time in Bali should catch one or two dance performances which are presented on regular schedules around the island. The performances are well-edited excerpts from the long, traditional Balinese dance-dramas. Entrance tickets usually range from Rp 1,800 to Rp 2,500. Some of the best dance performances are:

Barong and Kris Dance in three venues in Batubulan village, Gianyar, 9 a.m. every morning. Very theatrical and very popular.

Kecak Dance in Pura Ayodya, Tanjung Bungkak, Denpasar, also at the Art Center, Abian Kapas, both at 6 p.m. Both impressive and well staged.

Legong Dance at Puri Agung Stage in Peliatan, every Saturday, 6.30 p.m. A polished, popular performance. Also at Tirta Sari Stage, Peliatan, every Friday, 6.30 p.m. A good, creative show.

Mahabharatha Epic (a selection of dances), at Teges Stage, (by the silver dancer's statue), Peliatan, every Tuesday, 6.30 p.m. A particularly fine *gamelan* and dance group.

Trance Dance (derived from Sanghyang) in Bona, Gianyar, every Monday, Wednesday and Friday at 6 p.m. A dramatic selection of dances.

Ramayana Dance excerpts may be seen at regular dinner shows at the Hotel Bali Beach; Bali Hyatt; Sanur Beach Hotel and Nusa Dua Beach Hotel. Check hotel desk for times and venues.

The Frog Dance, *Topeng,* and *Joged* are popular shows, often hired to entertain large groups. Check with your hotel, tour agent, or nearby tourist restaurant for performance dates.

Driving

One should carry a valid International Driver's Permit or obtain one at the Traffic Police Office in Jln Supratman, Denpasar, for Rp 6,500. The fines for not having this licence on the road can be hefty. Cars keep to the left. Generally the roads are heavy with traffic, especially along the one-way streets in Denpasar. Once you are away from the busy roads of south Bali, navigation becomes easier. Most main roads have signposts but the actual driving remains "unnerving" and demands full attention.

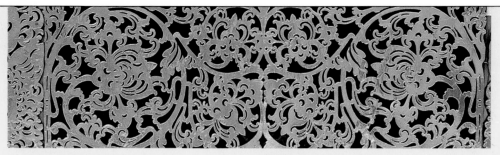

Drugs

The Bali authorities sternly warn tourists against the use of drugs. The penalties are high: several years in the Denpasar jail for a few grams of marijuana; a decade or two for a substantial quantity of hashish. Under Indonesian law even tourists who do not take drugs themselves, but know of others taking them, face jail if they do not report cases to the police.

Electricity

Denpasar, Sanur, Kuta and Ubud have 220 volts, 50 cycles. Other parts of Bali are still on 110 volts.

Emergencies

For Police, call 110. Thefts should be reported first to the hotel security office. Upon the loss of a passport, file a report immediately with the Police. For an ambulance, call 118 and 26305. The Public Hospital at Sanglah, Jln Diponegoro, Denpasar (tel. 24141 and 24142) receives patients 24 hours round the clock. There are hospitals and clinics in the major towns of Bali and reliable resident doctors at the major hotels like Hotel Bali Beach, Bali Hyatt, and Sanur Beach Hotel.

Essentials of Bali-Tripping.

As you explore, there are a few vital items you should carry with you **at all times** besides the usual good scout's pocket knife, flashlight, insect repellent, tissues and a few coins. **A cloth waist sash** is compulsory to wear when visiting temples. **A sarong** is useful since it is just not polite to bare one's legs in sacred places. Main temples will rent one for Rp 100-500 to cover up a tourist in shorts. It is usually better to wear a conservative, buttoned shirt than a singlet in your village-and-temple-venturing.

A relaxed attitude. Have a pleasant, open frame of mind. There will be aggressive vendors wherever you go (they are most persistent up in Kintamani). But the onus is on the tourist to be tolerant. Treat the "ritual" of bargaining like a game full of smiles and cajoling, not like a battle of "rip-offs"! And the pleasant spirit of Bali will stay with you. Bring a **camera and extra film,** but don't tip the "models". Begging is looked down upon by Balinese society so don't encourage the "hand-out" habit among the young scamps. (For extra special personal service, tip with a ballpen or T-shirt instead.) Finally, bring along a **simple map.** Most places in Bali are very accessible so you can't really get lost. If you have chartered a minibus and driver, it is all a matter of communicating clearly — pointing out your desired route — before you take off, especially if you are headed for the scenic villages that lie off the standard tour-guided routes.

Etiquette

While the Balinese may appear very relaxed about their way of life, they are a very correct people, living by a rigid code of conduct and adhering to a very polite social etiquette in dress and demeanor. They would never offer comment on the rude behavior of a foreigner, although they may be much offended. Therefore it is generally advisable to dress conservatively when visiting the villages and city offices. A collared shirt for the men; modest blouses for the women; and no shorts.

When entering a temple, it is compulsory to wear a waist sash, signifying respect in holy places. Some of the larger temples require the use of a sarong as well, which is rented out for a small fee. Women who are menstruating are asked not to enter temples. Visitors are quite welcome to witness the Balinese religious ceremonies and take photographs to their heart's content, provided they do not walk in front of people performing their prayers, nor climb upon the much-revered shrines.

Two particular taboos to watch: Never pat a person, even a child, upon the head, which is considered a sacred part of the body. And always remember to give and receive things, especially food, with the right hand only.

Festivals and Celebrations

The dates of festivals in Bali are determined by two complex and intermeshed calendars, the *wuku* and the *saka*. Big celebrations are held on the auspicious days of the 210-day Balinese year. But religious festivity is a daily habit. Visitors who ascertain the dates of Bali's movable festivals will catch some of the world's most unique and aesthetic celebrations.

Galungan

By the *wuku* calendar, Balinese celebrate the creation of the world and the victory of good over evil every 210 days. During Galungan, the most important holiday of the Balinese year, it is believed that all the deities and ancestral spirits descend from heaven and sojourn among their descendants. The 10-day festive season comes to a climax with Kuningan, when the gods and spirits are sent off after the prolonged visit to earth.

Nyepi

This is the Balinese New Year by the *saka* calendar, a holy day observed with complete stillness. No fires are lit, no transport is taken. On the day before Nyepi all the demons of the previous year are exorcised by purification sacrifices, by priests' recitations of mantras, and by loud noise which drives out evil spirits. On Nyepi itself, all Bali is silent. It is hoped that all demons will believe Bali "deserted and barren", and quickly leave the island.

Odalan

An *odalan* is a temple birthday or anniversary celebration, usually lasting three days. The entire village prepares for days, even weeks, to stage these sometimes phenomenal religious productions.

Tumpek Days

These are special days of honor set aside to celebrate specific individual gods or nature deities who are in charge of important aspects of a Balinese man's life. On the day honoring Dewi Saraswati, goddess of wisdom, offerings are made to her symbols of learning, especially to old *lontar* books. On **Pagerwesi**, which literally translates as "iron fence", prayers are offered for courage and strength to protect the family, the village and the world in general. On **Tumpek Landep**, offerings are made for metal tools, weapons, even cars and motorbikes. On **Tumpek Uduh** offerings are made for all plants and trees, which are suitably "dressed up" for the occasion. On **Tumpek Wayang,** the Balinese honor shadow puppets and theater masks.

Health

Come prepared with your own medicines for that most common ailment, the upset stomach known as "Bali Belly". The spicy food can cause a chronic case of diarrhoea, sure to ruin a vacation. Norit charcoal pills are available to calm a tender stomach. Lomotil, a prescription drug, seems to work fastest against the runs. Avoid unboiled water — stick to the bottled or packaged drinks, taken without ice. Wash all fresh fruit and vegetables well before eating. And when you get the inevitable scratches and bruises, use a good antiseptic and stay away from the sea. See page 76 for more remedies.

Hotels and Accommodation

Bali has accommodation to suit every pocket and every kind of visitor. At the top level of the market there are some 11,000 hotel rooms rated two-stars and above. These range from comfortable, moderately priced bungalows by the sea to the luxurious international standard resort complexes with pools, sports facilities, bars and restaurants. For the middle-level to low-budget tourist, there is a wide selection of *losmens* — inexpensive travelers' inns — located in the tourist towns. These run from a moderate U.S.$10–15 a night, down through the "cheap digs" costing U.S.$3–5. (Budget *losmens* are mainly in Kuta and Legian). "Home-stays" are the two or three rooms leased out within a family's own home — an often charming and reasonable arrangement commonly found in Ubud and the villages.

The following is a hand-picked list of accommodation choices in the prime tourist towns.

Luxury Class

Kuta
Pertamina Cottages (Tel. 25581)

Sanur
Bali Hyatt Hotel (Tel. 8271)

Nusa Dua
Nusa Dua Beach Hotel (Tel. 71210, 71215)
Hotel Bali Sol (Tel. 971510-20)
Hotel Putri Bali (Tel. 971020)

First Class

Kuta
Bali Oberoi Hotel (Tel. 25581)

Sanur
Bali Beach International (Tel. 8511)
Sanur Beach and Seaside Bungalows (Tel. 8011)
Segara Village (Tel. 8407, 8231, 8408)
Tandjung Sari Hotel (Tel. 8441)

Bungalow Class

Kuta
Kuta Beach Hotel (Tel. 25791)
Legian Beach Hotel (Tel. 26811, 26812)
Poppies Cottages (Tel. 23059)
Kuta Beach Palace (Tel. 25858)
Kuta Beach Club (Tel. 25056)

Sanur
Sindhu Beach Hotel (Tel. 8352, 8351)
Alit's Beach Bungalows (Tel. 8567, 8560)
Gazebo Cottages Beach Hotel (Tel. 8300)
La Taverna Bali Hotel (Tel. 8387)
Santrian Beach Cottages (Tel. 8181, 8182)

Denpasar
Bali Hotel (Tel. 25682, 25683)

Nusa Dua
Hotel Bualu (Tel. 71310, 71311)

Ubud
Hotel Tjampuhan
Puri Saren
Han Snel Bungalows

Moderate

Kuta
Sunset Beach Hotel (Tel. 24868)
Dyana Pura (Tel. 22914)
Mandara Cottage (Tel. 25765)
Agung Beach Inn (Tel. 26487)
Kuta Beach Club (Tel. 25056)

Sanur

Taman Agung Inn (Tel. 8549)
Laghawa Beach Inn (Tel. 8494)
Swastika Bungalow (Tel. 8573)

Denpasar

Hotel Denpasar (Tel. 26336)
Pemecutan Palace Hotel (Tel. 23471)

Hours

Balinese begin office work early — and end early. It is best to visit government offices, banks, and private businesses between 8 a.m. and 11.30 a.m. The usual hours of government offices are from 8 a.m. to 2 p.m. Monday to Thursday; 8 a.m. to 11.30 a.m. on Friday; and 8 a.m. to 12 midday on Saturday. Department stores in the capital follow suit, opening at 8 a.m. and closing around 1.30 p.m. then reopening at 5 p.m. after the heat has passed.

Language

Almost anywhere in Bali the people will speak Bahasa Indonesia, the Malay-based national tongue, along with their local Balinese dialect. English is widely spoken by those in tourism. Out in the villages some of the simple-to-learn Indonesian language will carry the visitor far. Pick up a few phrases — to ask directions and to bargain with — and the Balinese will respond with delight.

Money Matters

There are seven government banks in Denpasar and numerous money changers in the larger hotels and along the roads of Kuta and Sanur. Banks, open from 8 a.m. to 12 noon, Mondays to Fridays, and 8 a.m. to 11 a.m. on Saturdays, easily change major currencies (cash or traveler's checks) into rupiah, the official Indonesian currency.

Currency transactions receive faster attention in the private money-changers' offices. Bring along your passport. Visitors should carry small notes in the villages, where it is sometimes a major problem finding change for even a Rp5,000 note.

Museums

The Bali Museum in the heart of Denpasar (See Cultural Walking Tour) contains artifacts of Bali life and culture from prehistoric days to the present. The building itself is a fine example of Balinese palace and temple architecture. Open Tuesday to Thursday, 7.30 a.m. to 1.30 p.m.; Friday, 7.30 to 11.30 a.m.; Saturday and Sunday from 8 a.m. to 12.30 p.m. Closed Mondays.

The Werdi Budaya Art Center in Abian Kapas, Denpasar, displays a permanent collection of fine paintings and sculptures. Some items are also for sale. Open 8 a.m. to 5 p.m.

Museum Le Mayeur, in Sanur, on the north side of Hotel Bali Beach, contains the oil paintings of Belgian painter Le Mayeur du Perpres, who lived here from 1935 to 1958. The once-idyllic bungalow by the beach is still filled with images of his Balinese dancer-wife, Ni Pollok. Open daily till 2 p.m.

Museum Manusa Yadnya, in Mengwi by Pura Taman Ayun, is a display depicting Balinese "human being ceremonies"; shown are the varied palm-leaf offerings and decorations that accompany each family rite, as seen during birth, three-month birthday, tooth-filling ceremonies, etc. Open daily 8 a.m. to 2 p.m., closed Sundays.

Subak Museum, Kediri Road, Tabanan, is a new building on a hillside overlooking fields, containing the implements of the farmer and the farm household. Open daily 8 a.m. to 2 p.m., closed Sundays.

Gedong Kirtya Lontar Library, in Singaraja, North Bali, is a quiet repository of Bali's ancient learning as contained in some 6,000 *lontar* volumes, palm-leaf books that date back to the 13th century. Open every morning except Sundays.

Pejeng Archaeological Museum, Pejeng, Gianyar houses a collection of Megalithic and Bronze Age remains, plus stone sarcophagi. Open daily.

Museum Puri Lukisan in Ubud, displays the paintings and woodcarvings from Bali's modern artistic "renaissance" of the 1930s; plus excellent examples of contemporary art of the Ubud-Peliatan area. Some pieces for sale. Open 8 a.m. to 4 p.m. daily.

Photography

Bali is all geared up for shutter-bugs on holiday. Commercial photo service shops in Kuta and Sanur carry color film (Kodak and Fuji). Color print service is done efficiently within an hour. Transparencies take two days to process.

Private Transport

Beyond the tour agent's limo or the pricy hotel taxi, there are many forms of transport available to the enterprising visitor. Transport can be "chartered" by venturing out onto the Sanur or Kuta road, looking around for drivers hawking their vehicles, and simply negotiating your day's ride according to time, distance and type of vehicle. (See under Charter Transport, page 92).

If you do choose to do it yourself — and look for the remoter pleasures of Bali, here are guidelines:

Car Hire:

Rental cars are available from numerous car-hire agencies in Kuta, Sanur and Denpasar, for an average of U.S.$30 per day. Charges decrease as the days of rental increase. The most common vehicles available are the sturdy Suzuki jeep and the convertible-open-top Volkswagen Safari jeep.

Motorbike Rental:

Over 1,200 registered motorbikes are available for hire around Bali, mainly in Kuta and Sanur. The 125 cc bikes rent out at an average U.S.$3 a day; the large 175 ccs for U.S.$5. Rates decrease as rental time increases. You must carry an International Driver's Permit endorsed for motorbikes, registration papers, crash helmet, and bike insurance. And be warned that Bali's traffic police tend to specially scrutinize bike-riders at all times.

Bicycle Rentals:

Pedal power is the very best way to see Bali. See Tony Wheeler's *Bali and Lombok* guidebook before you take off. There are numerous pushbike rental shops in Kuta and Legian; bike parts and bikes for sale in Denpasar; and the cheapest bike-rentals in Ubud, at Rp1,000–1,500 per day.

Public Transport

Getting around Bali by mini-cabs (called bemos) or mini-buses is a cheap affair, running just Rp100–150 within a tourist town, and Rp250–350 into Denpasar, via the standard routes. It is best to ask a local about usual public *bemo* fares before you venture out, lest the drivers automatically charge you their "unaware tourist rates" — of five to ten times the normal public rate. Standard, up-to-date transport fares are usually posted on the wall at the Badung Tourism Office, in Denpasar.

Religious Services

There are a number of churches and mosques, located primarily in Denpasar. It is possible to find sites and hours through your tour agent or hotel desk. Catholic mass is served regularly on Saturdays in Sanur at 5 p.m. at the Bali Beach Hotel, 10th floor; and at 6 p.m. at the Bali Hyatt Hotel, Hibiscus Room. The city churches: Catholic, Jln Kepundung. Protestant, Maranatha, Jln Surapati. Seventh Day Adventist, Jln Surapati. Pentecostal, Jln Karna. Evengelical, Jln Melati. Protestant, Bali,

Jln Debes. Mosques: Raya Mosque, Jln Asanuddin; Al-Hissan Mosque, Hotel Bali Beach, Sanur.

Restaurants

Bali has developed a distinct world of small tourist restaurants (over 170 in Badung Regency, centered in Denpasar, Sanur and Kuta). Most carry a standard something-for-everyone menu composed of Western fare (steak, lobster, grilled fish or chicken), popular Indonesian dishes (*sate, nasi goreng,* fried noodles, *chap chai* vegetables) plus some Italian thrown in (spaghetti of course). Kuta Beach and the adjoining Legian have become something of a culinary mecca with a wide and interesting variety of tasty cuisines: Italian, Chinese, French, Mexican, Italian and fresh seafood grills. Sanur carries a range of Western tourist cuisine for a more upmarket clientele, along with one pricy Japanese restaurant. See also **Best Bets**.

Shopping

Bali is definitely a shopper's paradise when it comes to creative crafts, clothing and general holiday souvenirs. Bargaining is an inescapable — and, hopefully, enjoyable — part of the whole exchange; a clever shopper can get discounts of up to 50 per cent depending upon the time, place and situation. Area-wise, Kuta-Legian beach town is the liveliest shopping complex, with a great variety of goods arrayed in an endless string of small shops and big art markets. Denpasar carries a wide selection of goods in the department stores around Gajah Mada Street; prices are good, but hours are unusual — stores close from 1 p.m. to 5 p.m.

Best buys in Balinese arts and handicrafts include silver jewelry from Celuk; woodcarvings of dramatic masks or stylized statues from Mas; and Balinese decorative paintings from Ubud and Peliatan. See **Bali Tours**, **Arts and Crafts Trip**.

Best buys in cloth and clotning include the Balinese *endek* or local *ikat*-woven cloth; bright T-shirts and resort wear; and casual city clothes too.

Bali has lately become a central trading post for Indonesian ethnic arts and artifacts. Antique textiles from the other islands, primitive woodcarvings, baskets, and heritage jewelry are to be discovered amid the touristy souvenirs. See **Best Bets**.

Tipping

In the upmarket tourist world of fine hotels and restaurants a ten per cent tip is appropriate. Luggage bellhops expect Rp200–500 a piece. Outside, among taxi drivers and mid-budget restaurants, there is generally no tipping. Among the villages, a definite no again: monetary tipping is considered an insult among polite Balinese. Best to thank your host with a small present in lieu of cash.

Cultural museums and some artists' studios charge a minimal Rp200 entry fee. Some temples seek a small donation for upkeep; Rp200–500 per visitor is adequate. Within major temples, and other tourist attractions, there are sometimes freelance tour guides volunteering their services while you stroll about. Befriend them at your own discretion; you are under no obligation to pay a guiding fee.

Tours and Guides

There are some 30 registered tour agencies and about 10 to 12 standard tours offered around Bali. The price will depend on the agency, the number of persons booked for a tour, the transport, the time, etc. Some of the well-established tour agencies with tourist guides: Bali Indonesia Murni, Semawang, Sanur, (tel. 8464, 8434). Bali Tours, Jln Raya Sanur 130, Tanjung Bungkak, Dps, (tel. 24000). Jan's Tours & Travel, Br. Abian Kapas Kelod, Dps, (tel. 24595). Natrabu Tours & Travel, Jln Seruni 21, Dps, (tel. 25448, 25449). Pacto, Jln Hangtuah, Sanur, Dps, (tel. 8247, 8248). Rama Tours, Jln Raya Sanur 159, Dps, (tel. 24972, 23285).

Tourist Information Offices

The Bali Government Tourist Office at Renon Civic Center, on the south side of Denpasar, provides various tourist brochures, a map and calendar of events. Open Monday to Thursday 7.30 a.m. to 2.30 p.m. on Friday from 7.30 a.m. to 12 (tel. 22387). The provincial Badung Tourism Office on Jln Surapati by the big grassy square, Denpasar, provides up-to-date information and friendly advice; and the office is easier than the former to get to by public transport. Same hours, plus Saturday mornings till 12.30 p.m. (tel. 23602).

There's a tourist office at the Ngurah Rai International Airport (tel. 25081) and another at the Art Market in Kuta Beach. Bina Wisata, private tourist office operating in Ubud, provides the most up-to-date schedule of activities around the Gianyar regency and sells an amusing map of area walks.

Water

Foreigners are advised to drink only boiled or bottled water. Request bottled water at small restaurants or have a soft drink instead.

Index/Glossary